PRECIOUS PLANET

A User's Manual for Curious Earthlings

**ILLUSTRATED BY SARAH TAVERNIER &
ALEXANDRE VERHILLE
TEXT BY EMMANUELLE FIGUERAS**

TABLE OF CONTENTS

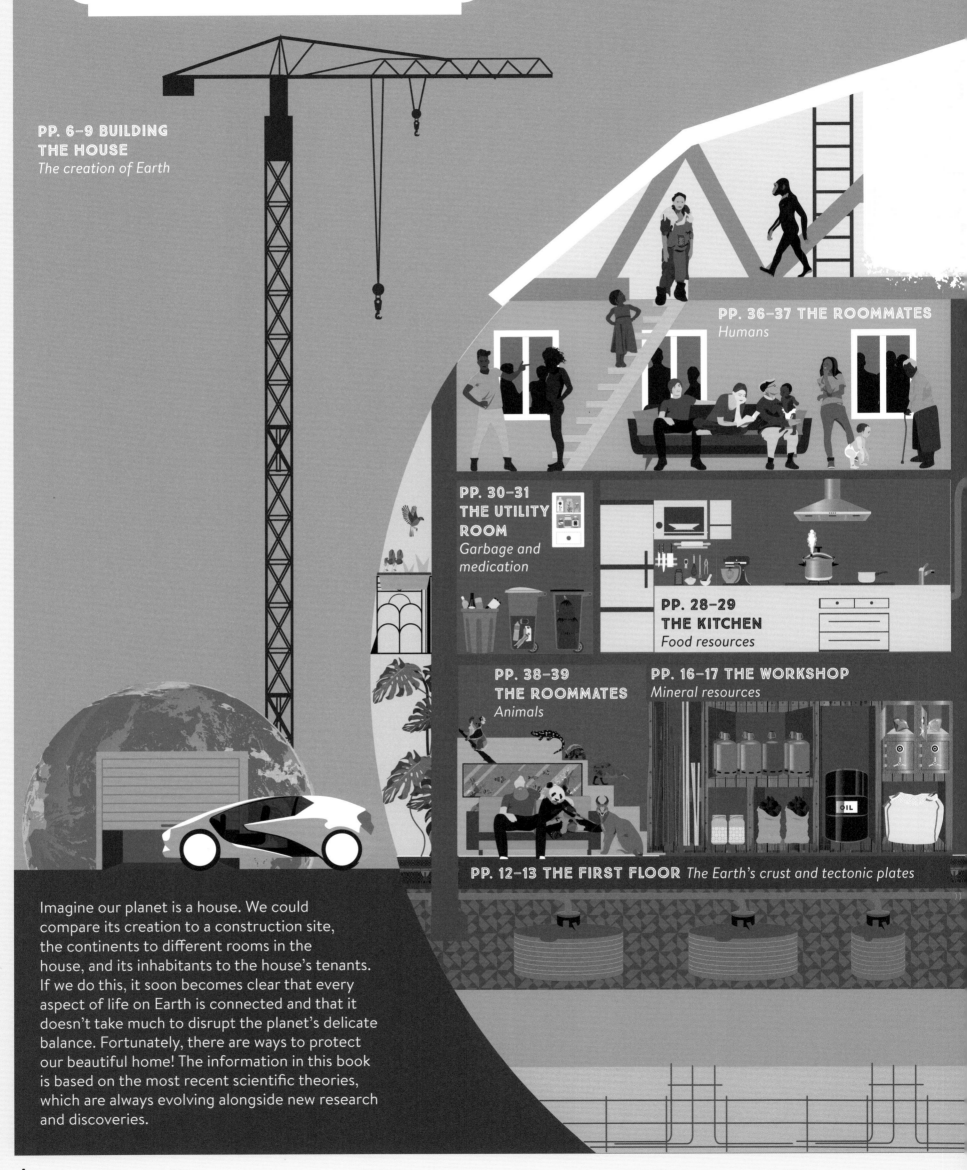

PP. 6–9 BUILDING THE HOUSE
The creation of Earth

PP. 36–37 THE ROOMMATES
Humans

PP. 30–31 THE UTILITY ROOM
Garbage and medication

PP. 28–29 THE KITCHEN
Food resources

PP. 38–39 THE ROOMMATES
Animals

PP. 16–17 THE WORKSHOP
Mineral resources

PP. 12–13 THE FIRST FLOOR *The Earth's crust and tectonic plates*

Imagine our planet is a house. We could compare its creation to a construction site, the continents to different rooms in the house, and its inhabitants to the house's tenants. If we do this, it soon becomes clear that every aspect of life on Earth is connected and that it doesn't take much to disrupt the planet's delicate balance. Fortunately, there are ways to protect our beautiful home! The information in this book is based on the most recent scientific theories, which are always evolving alongside new research and discoveries.

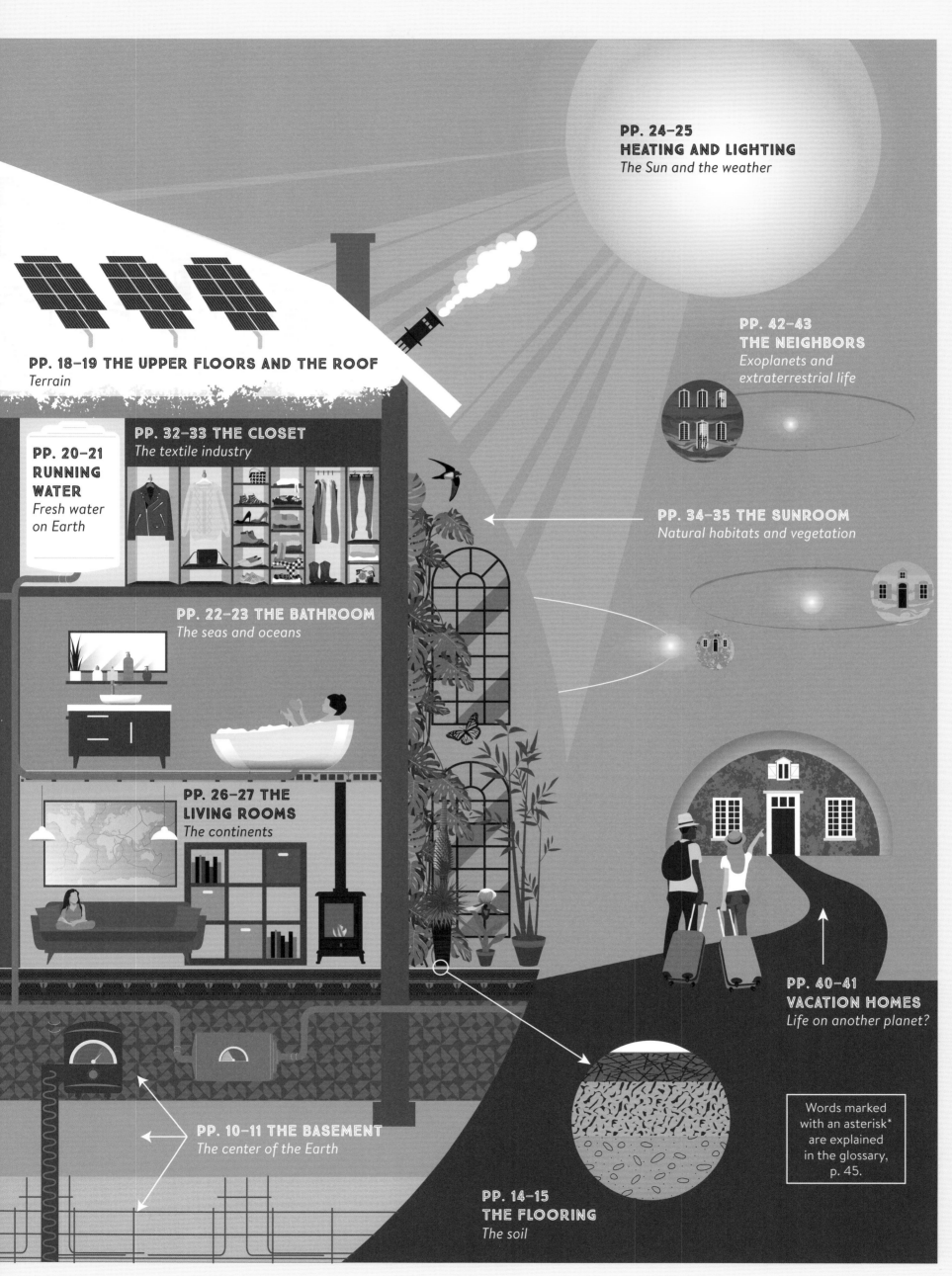

PP. 24–25
HEADING AND LIGHTING
The Sun and the weather

PP. 42–43
THE NEIGHBORS
Exoplanets and extraterrestrial life

PP. 18–19 THE UPPER FLOORS AND THE ROOF
Terrain

PP. 32–33 THE CLOSET
The textile industry

PP. 20–21
RUNNING WATER
Fresh water on Earth

PP. 34–35 THE SUNROOM
Natural habitats and vegetation

PP. 22–23 THE BATHROOM
The seas and oceans

PP. 26–27 THE LIVING ROOMS
The continents

PP. 40–41
VACATION HOMES
Life on another planet?

Words marked with an asterisk* are explained in the glossary, p. 45.

PP. 10–11 THE BASEMENT
The center of the Earth

PP. 14–15
THE FLOORING
The soil

BUILDING THE HOUSE

THE CREATION OF EARTH

BUILDING PERMIT

TITLE HOLDER: Universe & Co.

① **PROJECT DESCRIPTION**

ORIGIN:	Nobody knows when or how the Universe was created. Most scientists think that it all began with a giant explosion called the Big Bang.
NUMBER OF UNITS:	After that, galaxies began to form, made up of planets and stars.
TOTAL AREA:	Unknown.
PERMIT GRANTED:	13.7 billion years ago.
NUMBER OF CITIES:	There are at least 2 trillion galaxies in the Universe.

BIG BANG

THE BLUEPRINTS

②

☐ 1ST DRAFT: THE FLAT HOUSE

Up until the fifth century B.C., Greek philosophers believed that the Earth was shaped like a disk, surrounded by a river. Some thought it was sitting on a pillar, or that it was floating on water or in the air.

OCEAN
EUROPE
ASIA
LIBYA

☐ 2ND DRAFT: THE ROUND HOUSE

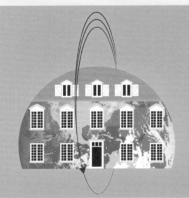

From the fifth century B.C. onward, most philosophers agreed that the Earth was round. If the stars look different depending on where you are in the world, it had to be because the Earth's curve stops us from seeing the whole sky!

EARTH'S CREATION LASTED NEARLY 40 MILLION YEARS.

☐ 3RD DRAFT: THE FLATTENED OVAL HOUSE

In the seventeenth century, scientists discovered the existence of gravity*, a force that pulls on and changes the shape of objects moving through space. As the Earth spins and orbits the Sun, it is subjected to a centrifugal force that flattens it at the North and South Poles—our planet isn't totally round!

7,926 MI. IN DIAMETER.

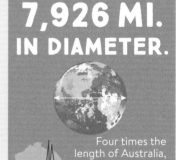

Four times the length of Australia, north to south.

☑ 4TH DRAFT: THE POTATO HOUSE

Pictures taken by satellites show that even though the Earth might look round from above, it is actually full of dents and bumps, like a potato!

SURFACE AREA OF THE EARTH:

197,000,000 SQ.MI.

= 52 × USA

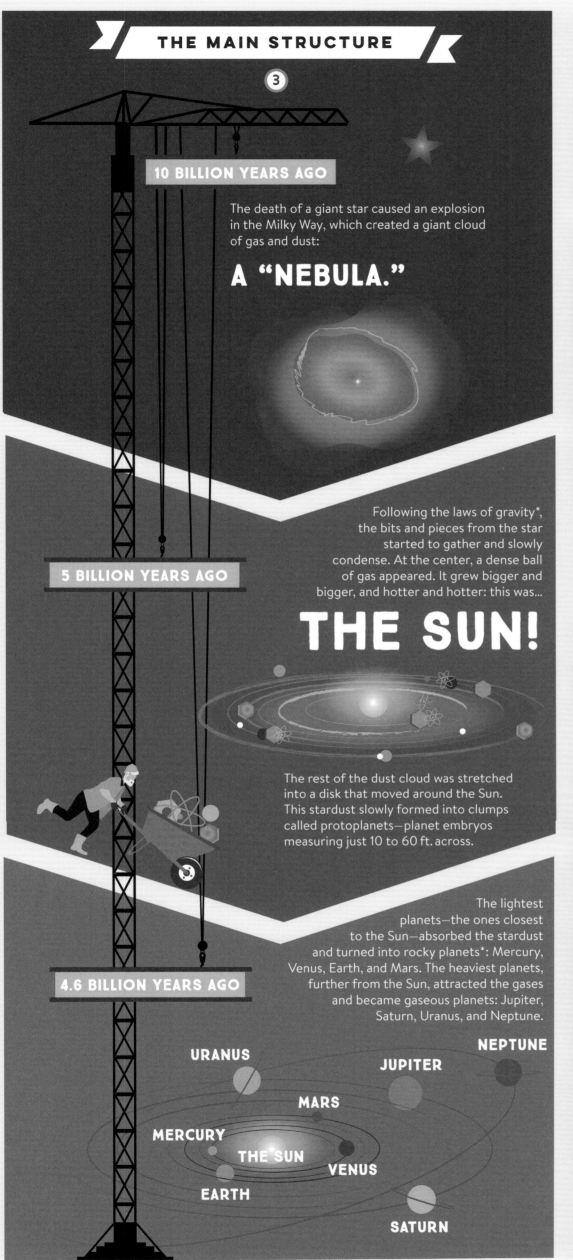

THE MAIN STRUCTURE

③

10 BILLION YEARS AGO

The death of a giant star caused an explosion in the Milky Way, which created a giant cloud of gas and dust:

A "NEBULA."

Following the laws of gravity*, the bits and pieces from the star started to gather and slowly condense. At the center, a dense ball of gas appeared. It grew bigger and bigger, and hotter and hotter: this was...

5 BILLION YEARS AGO

THE SUN!

The rest of the dust cloud was stretched into a disk that moved around the Sun. This stardust slowly formed into clumps called protoplanets—planet embryos measuring just 10 to 60 ft. across.

The lightest planets—the ones closest to the Sun—absorbed the stardust and turned into rocky planets*: Mercury, Venus, Earth, and Mars. The heaviest planets, further from the Sun, attracted the gases and became gaseous planets: Jupiter, Saturn, Uranus, and Neptune.

4.6 BILLION YEARS AGO

URANUS
NEPTUNE
JUPITER
MARS
MERCURY
THE SUN
VENUS
EARTH
SATURN

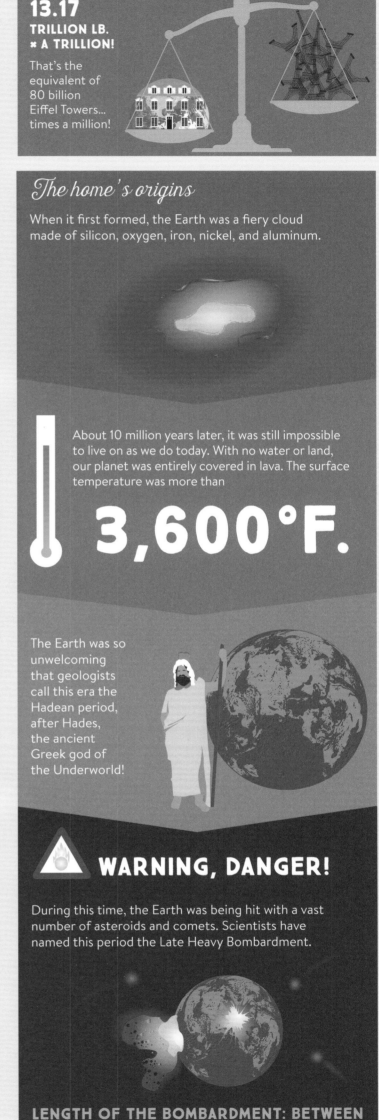

EARTH WEIGHS ABOUT
13.17
TRILLION LB.
* A TRILLION!

That's the equivalent of 80 billion Eiffel Towers... times a million!

The home's origins

When it first formed, the Earth was a fiery cloud made of silicon, oxygen, iron, nickel, and aluminum.

About 10 million years later, it was still impossible to live on as we do today. With no water or land, our planet was entirely covered in lava. The surface temperature was more than

3,600°F.

The Earth was so unwelcoming that geologists call this era the Hadean period, after Hades, the ancient Greek god of the Underworld!

⚠ WARNING, DANGER!

During this time, the Earth was being hit with a vast number of asteroids and comets. Scientists have named this period the Late Heavy Bombardment.

LENGTH OF THE BOMBARDMENT: BETWEEN
50 AND 150 MILLION YEARS.

NUMBER OF IMPACTS: 20,000 TIMES MORE THAN THE EARTH EXPERIENCES TODAY.

THE FINISHING TOUCHES

ABOUT 4.4 BILLION YEARS AGO, THE TEMPERATURE ON THE EARTH'S SURFACE FELL BELOW 570°F.

THE PLANET KEPT COOLING DOWN, AND ABOUT 3.5 BILLION YEARS AGO IT STARTED TO LOOK LIKE IT DOES TODAY.

THE ATMOSPHERE
The part of the cloud that stayed gaseous became the atmosphere, which was mainly composed of carbon dioxide at the time.

THE EARTH'S CRUST
The crust is made up of the lightest elements, such as silicon and aluminum, which floated up to the surface.

THE CORE
This is where the heaviest elements are found, such as iron and nickel.

THE OCEANS
Meteorites fallen to Earth combined with water from degassed* earthly matter. The oceans "only" took 150 million years to develop!

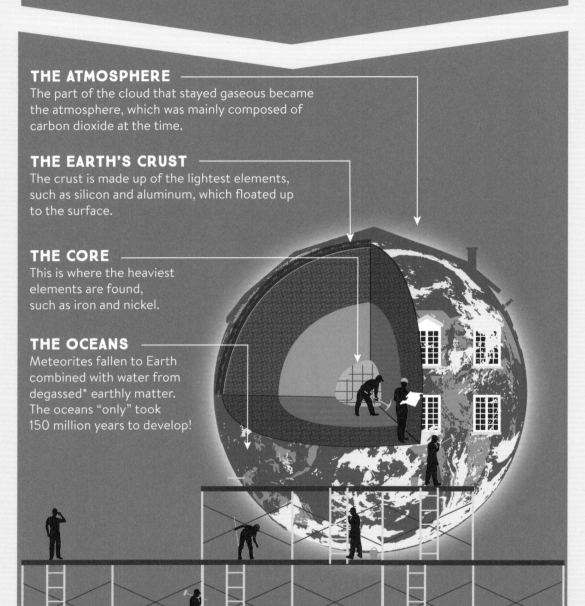

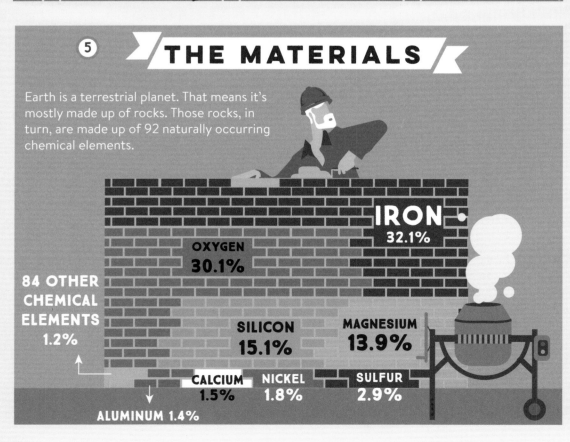

5 THE MATERIALS

Earth is a terrestrial planet. That means it's mostly made up of rocks. Those rocks, in turn, are made up of 92 naturally occurring chemical elements.

IRON 32.1%

OXYGEN 30.1%

84 OTHER CHEMICAL ELEMENTS 1.2%

SILICON 15.1%

MAGNESIUM 13.9%

CALCIUM 1.5%

NICKEL 1.8%

SULFUR 2.9%

ALUMINUM 1.4%

OUR HOME ADDRESS

6

The country

We don't know how the Universe is shaped, or how far it stretches, so it is difficult to know the exact location of the Milky Way. All we know is that it is situated in a cluster of galaxies called the Local Group, which consists of more than 40 galaxies.

The city

Our solar system is located in a large, spiral-shaped galaxy called the Milky Way. The glowing center is called the bulge. Enormous, star-studded arms spiral off from the bulge. The Sun is located in one of these arms, the Orion Arm, which is almost 30,000 light-years away from the center of our galaxy.

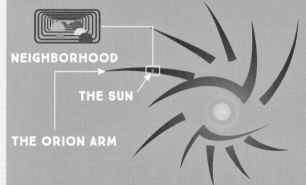

NEIGHBORHOOD

THE SUN

THE ORION ARM

The neighborhood

Our planet is part of the solar system. Our solar system consists of a star (the Sun), eight planets, their natural satellites, as well as dwarf planets and billions of celestial bodies (asteroids, comets, etc.).

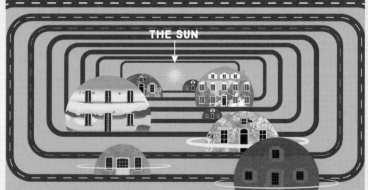

THE SUN

The street

The Earth is the third planet from the Sun, after Mercury and Venus.

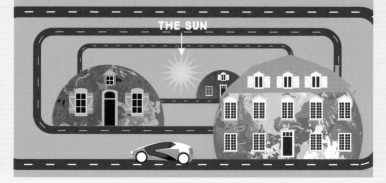

THE SUN

BUILDING THE GARAGE

⑦

4.35 billion years ago, the Earth was still very hot when it crashed into a small planet called Theia.

THE MOON IS THE EARTH'S ONLY SATELLITE.

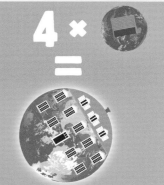

According to recent studies, scientists think it may have taken 20 collisions to create the Moon. But this theory is very recent and disputed.

The impact caused hot pieces of the Earth to fly off. These then gathered together and started orbiting around our planet.
THE MOON WAS BORN!

THE MOON MEASURES
2,158 MI.
IN DIAMETER. THAT'S SLIGHTLY MORE THAN A QUARTER OF THE EARTH'S DIAMETER:
7,926 MI.

4 × =

4 DAYS 7 HOURS:
That's how long Neil Armstrong and Buzz Aldrin took to complete the *Apollo 11* mission. On July 21, 1969, they became the first people ever to walk on the Moon.

THE TIME IT TAKES TO REACH THE MOON DEPENDS ON WHAT VEHICLE YOU USE.

⑧
THE DISTANCE BETWEEN THE HOUSE AND THE GARAGE

According to scientists, the Moon was less than
13,980 MI. FROM THE EARTH
when it was first formed.

But it keeps moving away—at the speed of 1.48 in. per year.

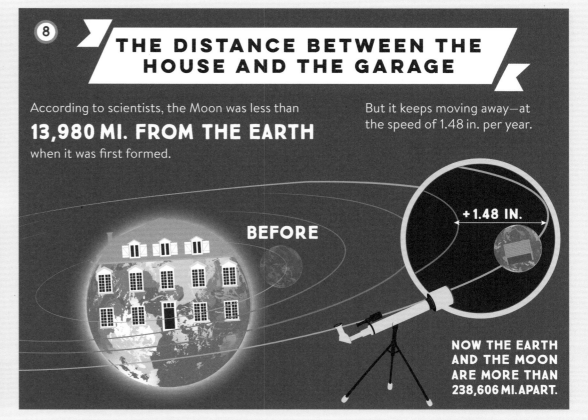

BEFORE

+1.48 IN.

NOW THE EARTH AND THE MOON ARE MORE THAN 238,606 MI. APART.

THE BLUE MARBLE

8 HOURS 35 MIN.:
The time it took the space probe *New Horizons*, launched from the rocket *Atlas V*, to travel between the Earth and the Moon in 2006.

DECEMBER 7, 1972:
The first clear photo to show the whole of our planet was taken by the crew of *Apollo 17*. They were about
28,000 MI.
away from the Earth.

The Moon travels at a speed of
2,288 MPH.
That's four to five times faster than a passenger plane!

⑨
A MOVING GARAGE

A moon is a celestial body that revolves around a planet. Our moon takes 28 days to complete its trip around the Earth.

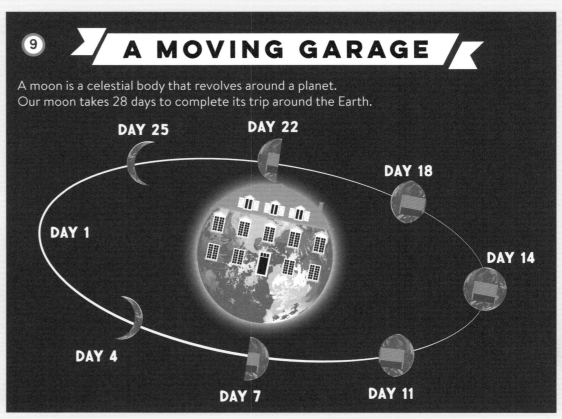

DAY 25   DAY 22

DAY 18

DAY 1

DAY 14

DAY 4

DAY 7   DAY 11

THE BASEMENT

THE CENTER OF THE EARTH

THE MANTLE ACCOUNTS FOR 82% OF THE EARTH'S VOLUME. THE CORE MAKES UP 16.5%.

① 1936: INGE LEHMANN

While she was studying the trajectories of seismic waves inside the Earth, a Danish earthquake specialist named Inge Lehmann discovered that the Earth has a solid inner core. Until then, everyone had assumed the core was completely liquid. In 1971 she became the first woman to receive the annual William Bowie medal from the American Geophysical Union.

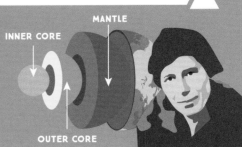
INNER CORE · MANTLE · OUTER CORE

② SELF-GENERATED ELECTRICITY

The inner core moves inside the metal liquid outer core. It rotates in the same direction as the Earth, but faster. The outer core rotates in the opposite direction. As the liquid metal moves, it generates an electric current and a magnetic field.

AVERAGE SPEED OF THE INNER CORE: 1,056 MPH

= 5 × AS FAST AS A RACE CAR

③ THE MOHO

1909: ANDRIJA MOHOROVIČIĆ

discovered the existence of a boundary between the mantle and the Earth's crust. The mantle is made of a rock called peridotite, but the boundary is made of granite and basalt rock. This boundary is called the Moho.

④ A TWO-STORY BASEMENT

THE MOHO

THE EARTH'S CRUST

The second level
Above the core, the mantle is formed of solid rocks called peridotites.

0 MI.
21 MI.
MANTLE
1,792 MI.
OUTER CORE

The first level
The core is composed of an inner and outer layer. The inner core is a solid ball of nickel and iron. This is surrounded by a liquid outer core made of molten metal.

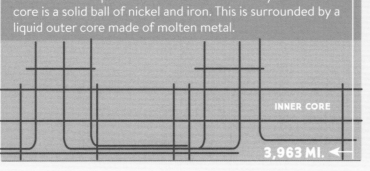

INNER CORE
3,963 MI.

THE INNER CORE IS THE SAME SIZE AS THE MOON.

⑤ THE BOILER

INSIDE THE EARTH, THE TEMPERATURE CHANGES DEPENDING ON HOW FAR DOWN YOU GO.

It's around 10,800°F in the inner core and roughly 6,000°F in the outer core. In the mantle, temperatures fluctuate between 7,000°F and 390°F, gradually decreasing until they reach an average of

59°F ON THE SURFACE OF THE GLOBE.

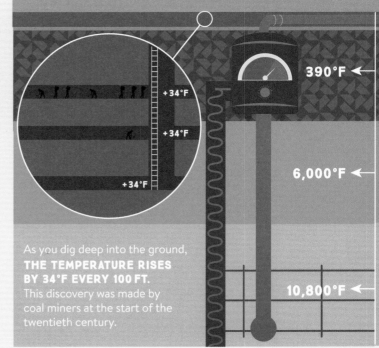

+34°F
+34°F
+34°F

390°F
6,000°F
10,800°F

As you dig deep into the ground, **THE TEMPERATURE RISES BY 34°F EVERY 100 FT.** This discovery was made by coal miners at the start of the twentieth century.

THE SECURITY SYSTEM

⑦

249 MPS: THE AVERAGE SPEED OF THE SOLAR WIND.

THE HOT WATER TANK

⑥

Is there an ocean in the middle of the Earth?

Scientists have discovered small amounts of water in certain kinds of rocks (ringwoodites) from deep inside the Earth's mantle.

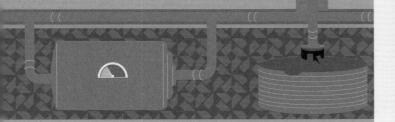

Although scientists don't know exactly how much water there is in the mantle, or how deep down it's hidden, they are sure that it exists.

OUR PLANET COULD CONTAIN A WATER RESERVOIR AS BIG AS ALL THE OCEANS COMBINED!

On position (shield in place)

The Earth is surrounded by a magnetic field that stretches more than 37,000 mi. into space. It acts as a protective shield by preventing the solar wind (particles from the Sun) from entering the atmosphere.

Medium position (shield is less effective)

The magnetic field is less effective at the poles, so the Sun's particles sometimes enter the atmosphere. When the particles come into contact with the gases in the air (oxygen, nitrogen, etc.), the gases begin to glow, creating bright streaks of colour (green, red, etc.). In the Northern Hemisphere, these lights are called the Aurora Borealis (or Northern Lights), and in the Southern Hemisphere, the Aurora Australis (or Southern Lights).

Off position (no shield)

The Earth would be exposed to the solar wind. Every second, the Sun emits millions of very strong particles. If they were to get into the Earth's atmosphere, they would disrupt satellites and GPS, and electrical devices on Earth. If the magnetic field did not exist, the fiery wind could make the oceans disappear and destroy all forms of life!

THE WARRANTY

⑧

THE EARTH'S OUTER CORE IS SLOWLY COOLING DOWN. What does this mean? It's solidifying at a rate of 1,000 tons per second and is growing by around 1/32 in. a year.

Scientists estimate that it will take the core several billion years to harden completely. So the magnetic shield should continue to protect us for a very, very long time!

THE FIRST FLOOR

THE EARTH'S CRUST AND TECTONIC PLATES

A FLOOR WITH TWO THICKNESSES

Sitting atop the mantle, the Earth's crust is broken up into several parts. Like a giant jigsaw puzzle, it's made up of 12 very large stone plates (as well as some other, smaller ones). These are the tectonic plates.

5 MI.

44 MI.

1. Thinner in the bathroom

The part of the Earth's crust found at the bottom of the ocean is called the oceanic crust. It is mostly made up of a rock called basalt and covers 70% of the Earth's surface. It is about 3 to 5 mi. thick.

2. Thicker in the living quarters

The continental crust, which the continents are made of, is composed of granite. It covers 30% of the Earth's surface and is between 9 and 44 mi. thick.

1/32 IN.:

THE THICKNESS OF THE EARTH'S CRUST IF OUR PLANET WERE A SOCCER BALL.

MORE THAN 80% OF EARTHQUAKES OCCUR IN AND AROUND THE PACIFIC OCEAN!

②
THE FLOATING FLOOR

Far below our feet, inside the Earth, the rocks that make up the mantle move and warp very slowly as they heat and cool. The hottest rocks rise and the coldest sink, creating a convection current. This causes the plates forming the Earth's crust to move—we call this plate tectonics.

1912:

The geophysicist Alfred Wegener developed the theory of plate tectonics. He realized that the continents are constantly moving and shifting under our feet!

THE FLOOR IS CRACKING

③

As they move, tectonic plates either collide, drift apart, or slip under one another. These movements put pressure on the plates, making them warp and buckle. When they reach a breaking point, they snap suddenly, causing violent jolts of varying strength.

THAT'S AN EARTHQUAKE!

THE SEISMOGRAPH

④

This tool measures the magnitude of an earthquake—it calculates how much energy it releases, on a scale of 0 to 9.5. The intensity of an earthquake is measured on the MSK scale, or the Medvedev-Sponheuer-Karnik scale (named after three European seismologists). This is a scale from 1 to 12, based on the effects felt by humans.

1 / 2	The earthquake can't be felt.
3 / 4	It causes small vibrations.
5	It wakes people up.
6	It moves furniture.
7	It leaves cracks in walls.
8 / 9	It causes houses to collapse.
10	It destroys bridges.
11 / 12	It destroys whole cities.

On average, **300 EARTHQUAKES** with a magnitude of 3 or more occur **EVERY DAY ON EARTH.** Fortunately, the vast majority of them are very weak and do not cause any damage!

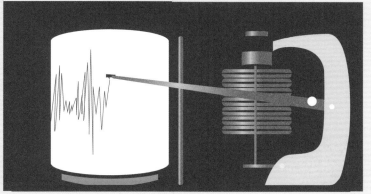

9.5: THE HIGHEST MAGNITUDE EVER RECORDED.

On May 22, 1960, in Chile, a violent earthquake destroyed the city of Valdivia and caused a tsunami. Waves several feet high traveled at up to 500 mph at sea before hitting the coast!

⑤ FINDING THE FAULT

Earthquakes occur along fault lines, which are cracks in the Earth's crust that occur mostly along the edges of two touching plates.

⑥ A WARPED FLOOR!

When two plates drift apart or when one slips under the other, magma (a mixture of gas and molten rock) can rise up, traveling from deep in the mantle all the way to the surface, creating a volcano.

⑦ CAN YOU PREDICT AN EARTHQUAKE?

And if the ground begins to shake, everyone knows what to do: hide under a table and stay away from windows. This helps you protect yourself from breaking glass and crumbling plaster.

No! We know the risk zones, but there's no way to predict earthquakes. So how can you protect yourself? In countries where earthquakes are more common (Chile, Japan, the United States, etc.), people build earthquake-resistant buildings that can handle shocks without collapsing.

THE FLOORING

THE SOIL

3 FT.
THE AVERAGE THICKNESS OF THE SOIL.

IT TAKES BETWEEN **100 AND 10,000 YEARS** FOR SOIL TO FORM.

THREE-PLY CARPET

①

UNDER THE VEGETATION, THE SOIL IS DIVIDED INTO THREE LAYERS, CALLED HORIZONS.

1. **THE ORGANIC HORIZON** (organic matter, such as decomposing leaves and animals).

2. **SURFACE SOIL** (a mixture of organic matter and minerals).

3. **SUBSOIL** (minerals such as sand, clay, etc.).

The horizons sit atop bedrock, the outer layer of the Earth's crust.

THE COLOR SAMPLE

The look and composition of different soils are determined by climate, the makeup of the Earth's crust below, the organisms the soil supports (animals, fungi, etc.), and human activities such as farming.

PEDOLOGISTS (SCIENTISTS WHO STUDY SOIL) DIVIDE SOIL INTO EIGHT DIFFERENT CATEGORIES.

②

SOIL CAPTURES **THREE** TIMES MORE **CARBON** THAN PLANTS DO!

Soils in Mediterranean regions (Greece, Spain, etc.). Often mineral-rich and fertile.

Soils in semi-arid regions (Benin, Mali, etc.). Contain low amounts of organic matter and are not very fertile.

Soils from coniferous forests in cold regions (Russia, Canada, etc.). Contain low amounts of organic matter and are not very fertile.

Soils in temperate forests (France, Germany, etc.). Very fertile and excellent for agriculture.

Iron-rich soils

Ferrallitic soils

Brown soils

Fersiallitic soils

Halomorphic soils

Isohumic soils

Podzols

Hydromorphic soils

Soils in equatorial and humid tropical regions (Brazil, Guyana, etc.). Very thick, mineral-rich, and fertile, but very fragile.

Soils from savanna areas (Kenya, Tanzania, etc.). Low in minerals and not very fertile.

Soils in wetlands in temperate regions (France, Germany, etc.). Waterlogged and not very fertile; they are often brown near the surface and grayish-green with patches of rust deeper down.

Soils from prairies in cold regions (Russia, Ukraine, etc.). Thick and very rich in organic matter, they are the most fertile in the world.

THE BATH MAT

③

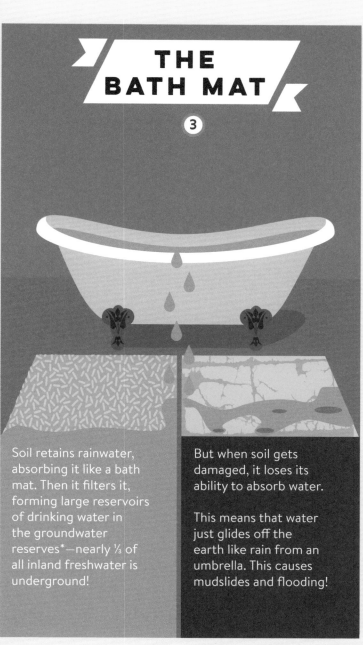

Soil retains rainwater, absorbing it like a bath mat. Then it filters it, forming large reservoirs of drinking water in the groundwater reserves*—nearly ⅓ of all inland freshwater is underground!

But when soil gets damaged, it loses its ability to absorb water.

This means that water just glides off the earth like rain from an umbrella. This causes mudslides and flooding!

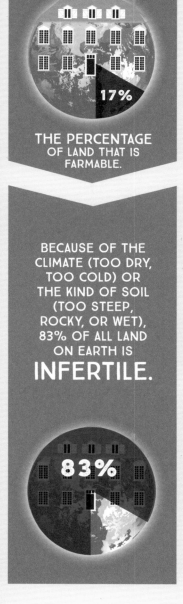

17%

THE PERCENTAGE OF LAND THAT IS FARMABLE.

BECAUSE OF THE CLIMATE (TOO DRY, TOO COLD) OR THE KIND OF SOIL (TOO STEEP, ROCKY, OR WET), 83% OF ALL LAND ON EARTH IS
INFERTILE.

83%

DUST MITES IN THE CARPET

④

Soil is a living environment where plants get the minerals they need and where humans grow food. It is also home to a vast range of animal life, with more than 3,000 species of earthworms, which are essential to maintaining its balance: without them, the soil would be quickly depleted. An impressive collection of species invisible to the naked eye also populates the underground world: mites, springtails, bacteria, fungi... All these organisms make the soil richer and more fertile.

¼

OF OUR PLANET'S BIODIVERSITY* LIVES UNDERGROUND.

A SINGLE SPOONFUL OF GARDEN SOIL CAN CONTAIN
OVER 1 MILLION ORGANISMS
SPREAD OVER SEVERAL THOUSANDS OF DIFFERENT SPECIES.

HOLES IN THE CARPET

⑤

Wear and tear

Over the past 100 years, the methods and products used in large-scale farming (pesticides, fertilizers, etc.), but also things like industrial waste, car traffic, construction (roads, housing, etc.), and waste (landfills, etc.), have polluted, depleted, eroded, and damaged the soil.

CONSEQUENTLY, more than 33% of the world's soils are now damaged.

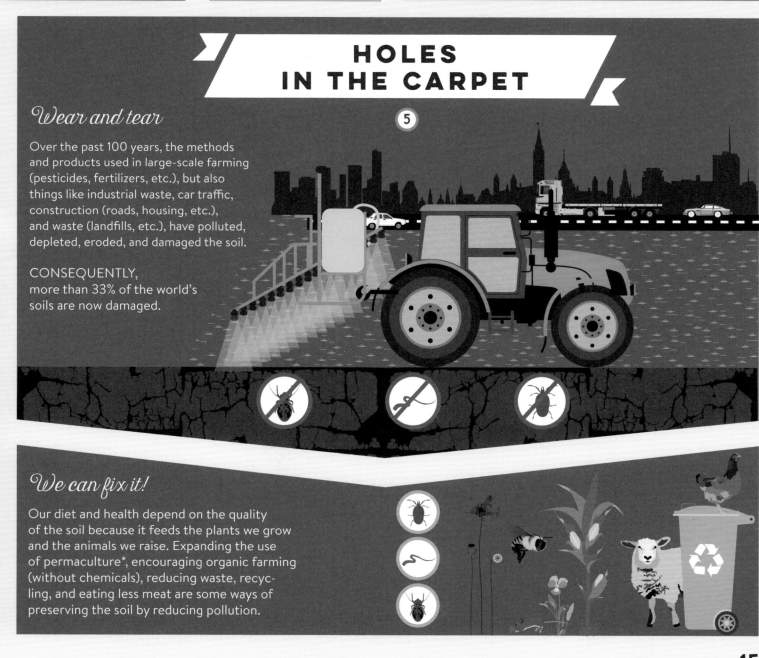

We can fix it!

Our diet and health depend on the quality of the soil because it feeds the plants we grow and the animals we raise. Expanding the use of permaculture*, encouraging organic farming (without chemicals), reducing waste, recycling, and eating less meat are some ways of preserving the soil by reducing pollution.

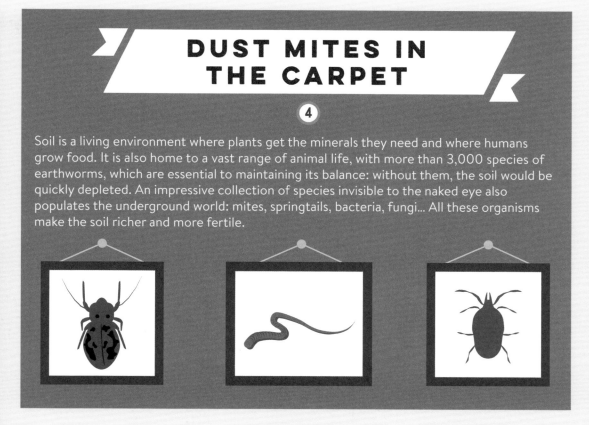

THE WORKSHOP

MINERAL RESOURCES

80:
THE MINIMUM NUMBER OF METALS REQUIRED TO MAKE A CAR.

METALS AND MINERALS

We use them to make most of our everyday objects (dishes, computers, car parts, etc.).

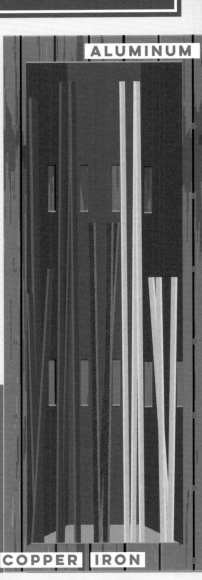

ALUMINUM

COPPER   IRON

BUILDING SUPPLIES

①

Just like a hardware store, the Earth's crust contains nearly everything we need to live comfortably: fossil fuels* (coal, oil, natural gas, etc.), rocks (limestone, marble, etc.), metals (iron, copper, etc.), and more than 4,000 minerals (quartz, kaolinite, calcite, etc.).

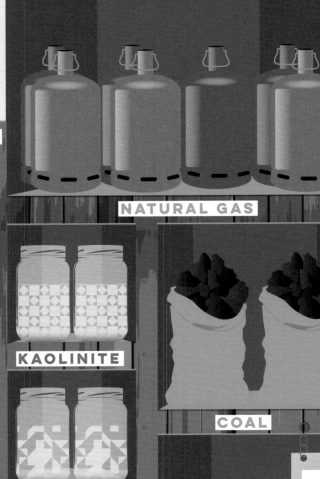

NATURAL GAS

KAOLINITE

QUARTZ

CALCITE

COAL

FOSSIL FUELS*

Used to make gasoline, heat our homes, and produce electricity.

OIL

OIL

ROCK

Used to build roads, bridges, and homes.

MARBLE   LIMESTONE

LOW SUPPLIES?

②

FOSSIL FUELS*

Caused by living organisms (mostly plants) decomposing over millions of years, these fuels are limited and nonrenewable. That means that once we use them all up, they will be gone forever.

OUT OF SUPPLIES IN 50 YEARS

The world's supply could run out in about 150 years.

METALS AND MINERALS

Metals (zinc, copper, lead, silver, etc.) only exist in limited quantities. Because of constant mining, natural deposits are running out.

OUT OF SUPPLIES IN 25 YEARS

LEAD

The world's supply could run out in about 20 years.

NATURAL GAS   OIL   COAL   COPPER   ZINC

THE VAULT

The rarest and most valuable rocks are called gemstones. We use them in jewelry and there are four main types. Each is formed in the Earth's mantle.

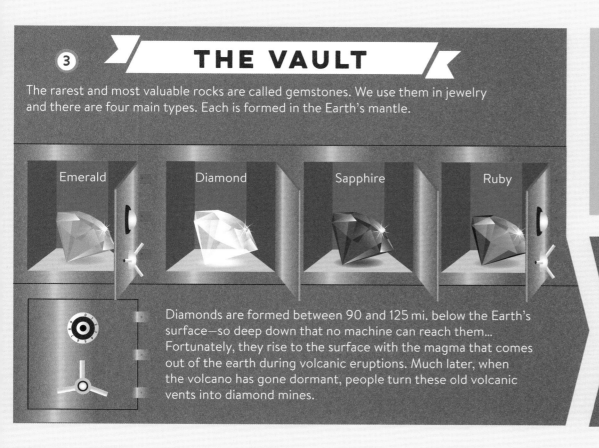

Emerald   Diamond   Sapphire   Ruby

Diamonds are formed between 90 and 125 mi. below the Earth's surface—so deep down that no machine can reach them... Fortunately, they rise to the surface with the magma that comes out of the earth during volcanic eruptions. Much later, when the volcano has gone dormant, people turn these old volcanic vents into diamond mines.

KEEP THINGS CLEAN! ⑤

The problem: fossil fuels *

Oil, natural gas, and coal are convenient to use. But when they are burned they release particles that pollute the atmosphere and make our climate dangerously warm.

3 BILLION YEARS.

That's how old the diamonds are that were found in some South African mines.

An example: aluminum

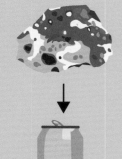

1. The aluminum you find in soda cans is made from a rock called bauxite. Unfortunately, there's a limited supply of bauxite, and mining it pollutes the environment.

REPLENISHING SUPPLIES ④

Even if supplies run out, all the metal found in everyday objects (soda cans, computers, mobile phones, televisions, etc.) can be recycled and used again. By recycling, we can conserve our natural reserves and reduce mining, which causes lots of pollution.

2. This is why we throw our aluminum cans in the recycling bin.

3. The cans are brought to a processing plant, where they are melted down. The molten aluminum is then turned into very thin sheets.

The solution: renewable energy

The Sun, wind, water, and the Earth's warmth can be used to heat our homes or produce electricity. Solar, wind, hydro, and geothermal power produce very little pollution and can be used over and over without running out. Considered the energy solutions of the future, they are becoming more and more common all over the world.

4. Then the recycled metal can be used to make a bike frame, a car part... or new soda cans!

670 RECYCLED SODA CANS

= 1 BIKE FRAME

THE UPPER FLOORS AND THE ROOF

TERRAIN

① THE ROOF

High-altitude mountains are the youngest, since they have very high, jagged peaks that haven't been smoothed down by erosion* yet. This is the case with the Alps, the youngest and tallest mountains in Western Europe, born about 44 million years ago.

MONT BLANC IS THE HIGHEST POINT IN THE ALPS.

3 MI.

② THE FLOORS

ALMOST 90% OF POLAND IS LOCATED LESS THAN 650 FT. ABOVE SEA LEVEL.

The country's name reflects this unique geographic feature. It comes from the name of a tribe, the Polans, which literally means "people of the plain."

A TOPOGRAPHIC MAP OF POLAND

- ◼ Higher than 2,000 ft.
- ◻ From 650 to 2,000 ft.
- ◻ Less than 650 ft.

The third floor and the attic

Mountains cover nearly ¼ of the Earth's surface. But the taller the mountain, the lower the number of people who live on it. Only 10% of the world's population lives on mountains! Only 8% of humanity has made a home at an altitude of higher than 3,200 ft., and only 1.5% lives higher than 6,500 ft. Less than 1% of the world's population lives higher than 8,200 ft.!

ANYTHING HIGHER THAN 2,000 FT.

is considered a mountain. These enormous rock formations typically have steep slopes and high peaks. Older mountains have rounder slopes that have been blunted by erosion*.

The second floor

Plateaus are higher than plains and are flat expanses of land, generally between 650 and 2,000 ft. above sea level. Plateaus are often carved into by deep valleys and canyons that are hard to cross without a bridge or a viaduct.

PLAINS + PLATEAUS = ¾ OF THE CONTINENTS.

2,000 FT.

The first floor

Plains are flat or slightly hilly stretches that are less than 650 ft. above sea level. They are often located near the sea and there is typically a river that flows through them. These features make them the perfect place for growing food, building a home, and getting around. That would explain why **MORE THAN 50% OF THE WORLD'S POPULATION** calls the plains home.

650 FT.

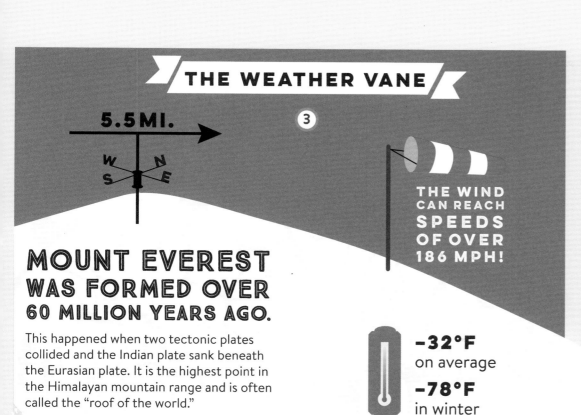

THE WEATHER VANE ③

5.5 MI.

THE WIND CAN REACH **SPEEDS OF OVER 186 MPH!**

MOUNT EVEREST WAS FORMED OVER 60 MILLION YEARS AGO.

This happened when two tectonic plates collided and the Indian plate sank beneath the Eurasian plate. It is the highest point in the Himalayan mountain range and is often called the "roof of the world."

-32°F on average
-78°F in winter

④ THE CHIMNEY

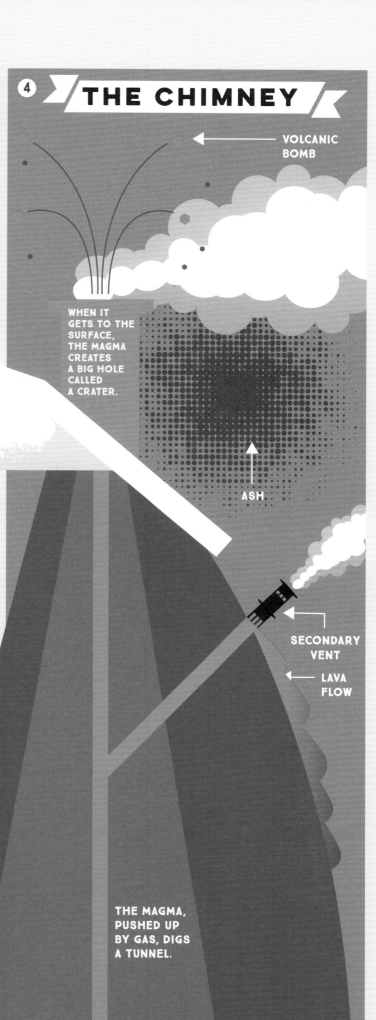

VOLCANIC BOMB

WHEN IT GETS TO THE SURFACE, THE MAGMA CREATES A BIG HOLE CALLED A CRATER.

ASH

SECONDARY VENT

LAVA FLOW

14:

THE ESTIMATED NUMBER OF SUMMITS HIGHER THAN 26,000 FT.

Mount Everest, K2, Kangchenjunga, Lhotse, Makalu, etc.

They're all located in the Himalayan mountain range on the border between China, Pakistan, Nepal, and India.

1,670:

The approximate number of active volcanoes on Earth. All of them have erupted at least once in the past 10,000 years!

18 LB. OF TRASH:

How much every climber must bring back before they can get back the money they had to give as a deposit to climb Mount Everest.

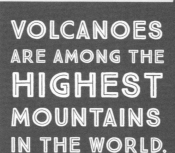

VOLCANOES ARE AMONG THE HIGHEST MOUNTAINS IN THE WORLD.

THE MAGMA, PUSHED UP BY GAS, DIGS A TUNNEL.

Mount St. Helens

On May 18, 1980, this volcano erupted and ejected nearly 24 cu. mi. of magma. The explosion was so violent that it destroyed the surrounding forest for hundreds of miles. The volcano collapsed in on itself. With its peak gone, the mountain suddenly became 1,314 ft. shorter in under 5 minutes.

This policy was put in place by the Nepalese government in order to clean up the mountain, which has been polluted by tons of waste (oxygen cylinders, ropes, etc.) since the summit was first reached in 1953.

As long as they are active, volcanoes are living mountains: they can spit out different materials (rocks, ash, lava, etc.), and their peaks can explode and/or collapse during an eruption.

VOLCANIC VENT

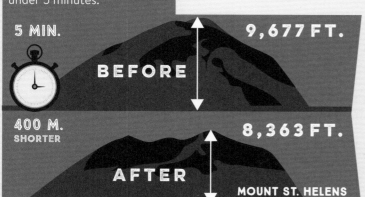

5 MIN.

400 M. SHORTER

9,677 FT.
BEFORE

8,363 FT.
AFTER

MOUNT ST. HELENS

AN ERUPTING VOLCANO

THE EARTH'S CRUST

MAGMA CHAMBER

0 TO 19 MI.   MANTLE

RUNNING WATER

FRESH WATER ON EARTH

MORE THAN 1 MILLION MI.:

THE TOTAL LENGTH OF PIPES **THAT SUPPLY DRINKING WATER TO THE USA.**

1 OUT OF 3 PEOPLE IN THE WORLD DON'T HAVE ACCESS TO SAFE DRINKING WATER.

TAP WATER
1

SEEN FROM SPACE, THE EARTH IS BLUE. SEAS AND OCEANS COVER 71% OF THE EARTH'S SURFACE.

71%

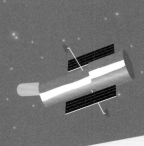

NOT ALL THIS WATER CAN BE USED BY HUMANS.

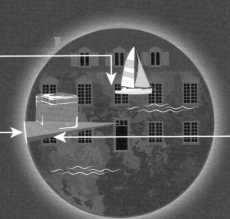

SALT WATER: 97%

FRESH WATER: 3%
¾ of the world's fresh water is frozen, in glaciers and icebergs at the North and South Poles.

0.7%
That means only ¼ of the freshwater supply can be used by humans. This water is found in rivers, lakes, or groundwater reserves*.

THE PIPES
2

The first circuit
Fresh water is first taken from a stream or a groundwater reserve* located in the Earth's crust. Then it travels through a pipe to a water plant, where it is treated to make it safe to drink. Then it gets tested and delivered to the pipes in our homes.

THE DRINKING WATER IN OUR HOMES COMES FROM **GROUNDWATER RESERVES*** AND **FRESHWATER SOURCES** SUCH AS RIVERS AND STREAMS.

0.7%:

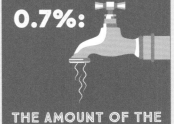

THE AMOUNT OF THE EARTH'S FRESH WATER THAT WE CAN USE.

The second circuit
In the other direction, the water we use at home (laundry, toilets, cooking, etc.) goes back to a wastewater-treatment plant before being released into the environment. In many poor countries, though, wastewater is poured back untreated.

RENEWABLE SUPPLIES

2. As it cools, the water vapor condenses into small drops to form clouds.

3. Then the water falls back to Earth in the form of rain or snow, replenishing the glaciers and groundwater reserves*!

1. The Sun's heat causes water to evaporate from oceans, lakes, and rivers. The water vapor builds up in the atmosphere.

There isn't much freshwater in the world, but our supply is constantly being replenished.

WHAT IS FRESH WATER USED FOR?

FARMING USES **70% OF THE FRESH WATER** THAT WE CONSUME FOR WATERING **CROPS.**

IN FACTORIES

20% OF FRESH WATER IS USED FOR INDUSTRIAL PURPOSES.

FOR DRINKING, COOKING, SHOWERING, ETC...

10% OF FRESH WATER IS CONSUMED BY PEOPLE.

WATER OUTAGES

Some parts of the world receive a lot of rain and/or snow, while others are affected by drought. Because of this, not all countries have the same freshwater reserves.

More than half of the world's freshwater supply is concentrated in just nine countries: Brazil, Russia, the United States, Canada, China, Indonesia, India, Colombia, and Peru.

By contrast, Israel, Kuwait, Jordan, and the United Arab Emirates have virtually no freshwater reserves. Each person there has 160 times less water than a Canadian person!

USING LESS WATER

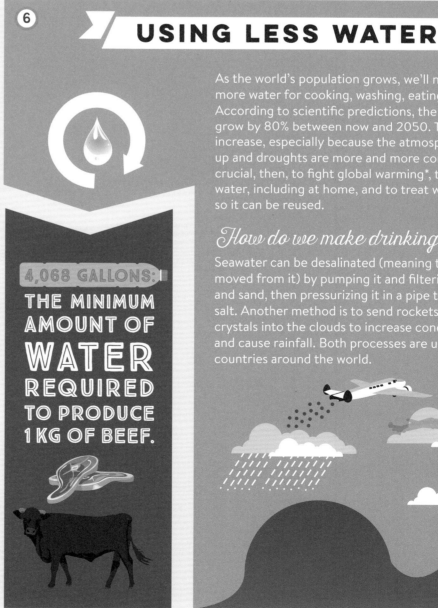

As the world's population grows, we'll need more and more water for cooking, washing, eating, and drinking. According to scientific predictions, the population could grow by 80% between now and 2050. This is a huge increase, especially because the atmosphere is heating up and droughts are more and more common! It is crucial, then, to fight global warming*, to use less fresh water, including at home, and to treat wastewater so it can be reused.

How do we make drinking water?

Seawater can be desalinated (meaning the salt is removed from it) by pumping it and filtering out the algae and sand, then pressurizing it in a pipe to remove the salt. Another method is to send rockets filled with salt crystals into the clouds to increase condensation* and cause rainfall. Both processes are used in several countries around the world.

4,068 GALLONS: THE MINIMUM AMOUNT OF **WATER** REQUIRED TO PRODUCE 1 KG OF BEEF.

THE BATHROOM

THE SEAS AND OCEANS

The five oceans (Pacific, Atlantic, Arctic, Southern, and Indian) and dozens of seas (Mediterranean, Black Sea, Red Sea, etc.) form a single global ocean.

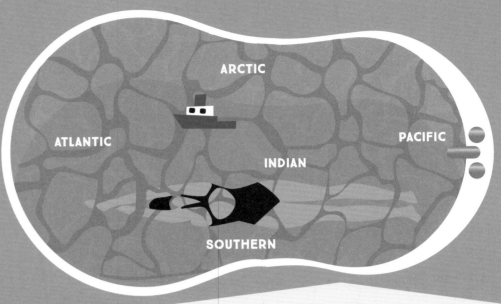

ARCTIC

ATLANTIC

PACIFIC

INDIAN

SOUTHERN

High-tech options

THE AIR PURIFIER:

The ocean captures nearly 30% of the carbon dioxide (CO_2) humans produce each year. CO_2 is a major contributor to global warming*. Thankfully, there are microscopic algae (phytoplankton) that absorb this toxic gas and transform it into the oxygen (O_2) we need to breathe. Another helpful factor is that CO_2 naturally dissolves in the oceans' cold waters.

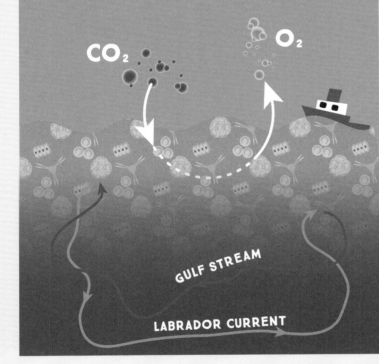

CO_2 O_2

GULF STREAM

LABRADOR CURRENT

A healthy ocean is essential to the well-being of our planet and our existence. That's why it's so important to take care of it!

THE GLOBAL OCEAN
=
MORE THAN 138,000,000 SQ. MI.
ALMOST 326 MILLION CU. MI. OF WATER
12,100 FT. DEEP ON AVERAGE

The deepest point is about 36,070 ft. below the surface. It's located in the Mariana Trench in the Pacific Ocean.

THE JACUZZI:

Ocean currents are constantly moving huge amounts of water through the ocean. They can be cold (Labrador, Oyashio, etc.), or hot (Gulf Stream, Kuroshio, etc.) and can be dozens of miles wide and thousands of miles long.

THE TEMPERATURE REGULATOR:

The ocean is also the Earth's most important climate regulator. It absorbs a huge amount of the Sun's heat, transports it using ocean currents, and redistributes it into the atmosphere!

② BE AWARE OF THE BATH'S TEMPERATURE!

Because of global warming*, the temperature of the oceans and seas is rising. This is making scientists very worried.

The warmer the water, the stronger the hurricanes and cyclones! As they form over the ocean, they get their strength from evaporating water. These huge tropical storms have become more powerful and destructive than ever before.

Warmer waters, combined with pollution, also lead to lower levels of oxygen in the ocean. This creates dead zones where marine species suffocate to death if they cannot escape.

AN OVERFLOWING BATHTUB

3

3 FT.: THE AMOUNT THE OCEANS COULD RISE BY 2100.

The higher the ocean temperature climbs, the higher the sea level rises! Not only because hot water takes up more space than cold water, but also because when glaciers melt it increases how much water is in the sea... Sea levels rose by 8 in. in the twentieth century.

The problem is that, as the sea rises, it could eat away at beaches and coastlines, flood cities, and swallow up islands. It could also seep into our groundwater reserves*, making them salty. There would then be less drinking water, which would force millions of people to leave their home countries.

DIRTY BATHWATER

4

It's not an accident that more and more companies and manufacturers are looking to cut back on making plastic items as a way of fighting against ocean pollution. A huge amount of bottles, wrappers, and other plastic waste is carried by ocean currents. This leads to large floating dumps, where the trash has merged. From the Pacific to the North Atlantic, several "plastic soups" or "garbage patches" have been discovered, where gyres—giant whirlpools in the ocean—occur.

THESE ARE BEING CALLED THE SEVENTH CONTINENT.

GOAL FOR 2050: NOT TO HAVE MORE PLASTIC IN THE OCEAN THAN FISH!

How do we remove plastic waste from the ocean? One of the many ideas that scientists have proposed came from a young inventor who designed floating barriers fitted with nets. These nets are able to collect huge amounts of sea waste.

THE GREAT PACIFIC GARBAGE PATCH IS **3 TIMES** THE SIZE OF FRANCE AND CAN REACH DEPTHS OF **100 FT.!**

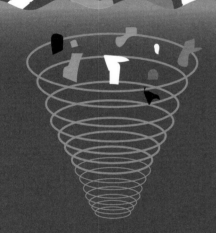

1 MILLION BIRDS AND 100,000 MARINE MAMMALS ARE KILLED EACH YEAR BY AQUATIC WASTE.

THE TOILET

5

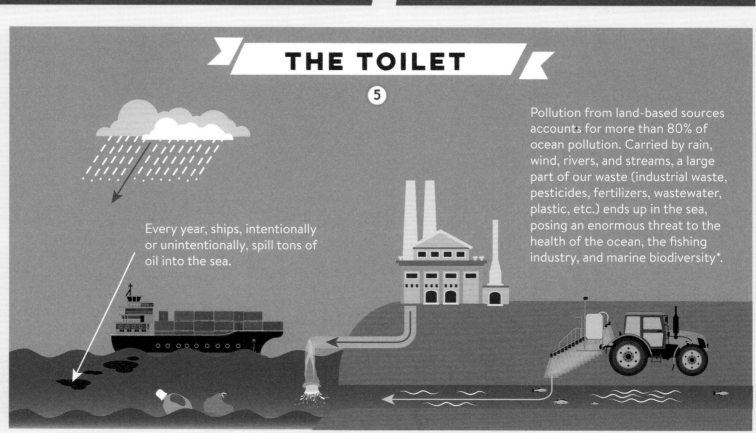

Every year, ships, intentionally or unintentionally, spill tons of oil into the sea.

Pollution from land-based sources accounts for more than 80% of ocean pollution. Carried by rain, wind, rivers, and streams, a large part of our waste (industrial waste, pesticides, fertilizers, wastewater, plastic, etc.) ends up in the sea, posing an enormous threat to the health of the ocean, the fishing industry, and marine biodiversity*.

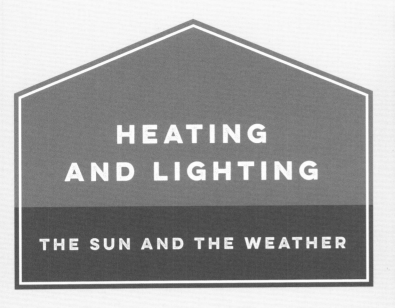

HEATING AND LIGHTING

THE SUN AND THE WEATHER

THE SUN'S DIAMETER IS 100 TIMES GREATER THAN THE EARTH'S.

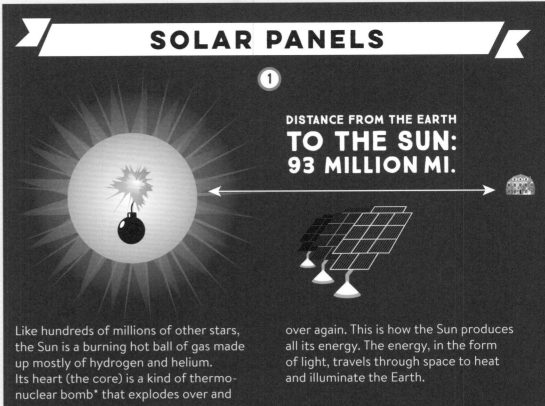

SOLAR PANELS

1

DISTANCE FROM THE EARTH TO THE SUN: 93 MILLION MI.

Like hundreds of millions of other stars, the Sun is a burning hot ball of gas made up mostly of hydrogen and helium. Its heart (the core) is a kind of thermo-nuclear bomb* that explodes over and over again. This is how the Sun produces all its energy. The energy, in the form of light, travels through space to heat and illuminate the Earth.

THE THERMOSTAT

How-to guide

2

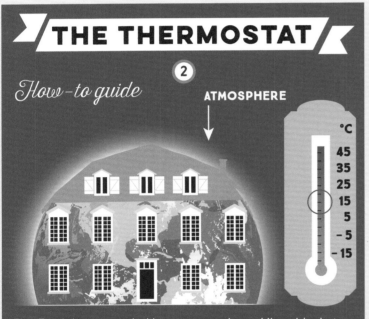

ATMOSPHERE

°C
45
35
25
15
5
-5
-15

The Earth is surrounded by an atmosphere. Like a blanket, it retains the Sun's heat. This process is known as the greenhouse effect. Because of it, the average temperature of our planet is 59°F. Without the atmosphere, it would drop to about -1°F, and the Earth would be covered in ice!

2018 WAS ONE OF THE WARMEST YEARS SINCE 1880. THAT YEAR, THE EARTH'S TEMPERATURE WAS

1.5°F

hotter than average. That's not much, but it's enough to disrupt the environment.

27 MILLION°F: THE TEMPERATURE OF THE SUN'S CORE.

ON THE SURFACE IT'S "ONLY" 9,932°F.

Solutions

According to scientists' predictions, the Earth's temperature could increase by 5°F–9°F by 2100. This would have catastrophic effects. Because of this, most countries have made a commitment to limit the production of greenhouse gases*. Fortunately, there are a lot of solutions: reduce transport, recycle more and burn less waste, and develop cleaner energy sources (solar, wind, etc.) so as to rely less on fossil fuels* (oil, coal, etc.).

Malfunctioning

The Earth naturally emits different greenhouse gases* (water vapor, methane, carbon dioxide, etc.) that help it maintain its average temperature. But human activities (burning fossil fuels*, driving cars, manufacturing, raising livestock, etc.) also produce a lot of greenhouse gases*. When the concentration of these gases increases in the atmosphere, the Earth's temperature goes up and the climate changes. This leads to drought, famine, fires, floods, hurricanes, cyclones, water shortages, the melting of glaciers, a rise in sea levels, and a mass extinction of species. These are some of the main effects of global warming*.

+5°F–9°F

2019 → 2100

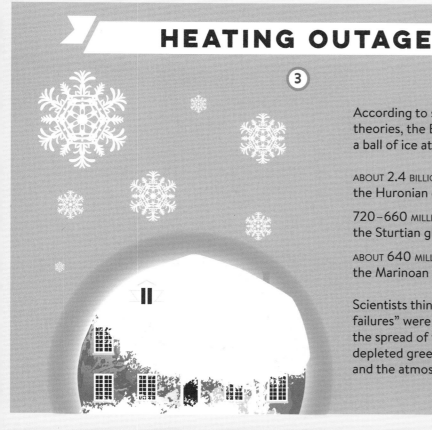

HEATING OUTAGE

③

According to some scientific theories, the Earth has turned into a ball of ice at least three times.

ABOUT 2.4 BILLION YEARS AGO: the Huronian glaciation.

720–660 MILLION YEARS AGO: the Sturtian glaciation.

ABOUT 640 MILLION YEARS AGO: the Marinoan glaciation.

Scientists think these "heating failures" were caused by the spread of tiny bacteria that depleted greenhouse gases* and the atmosphere.

④

THE LIGHTING

67,000 MPH: THE AVERAGE SPEED THE EARTH REVOLVES AROUND THE SUN.

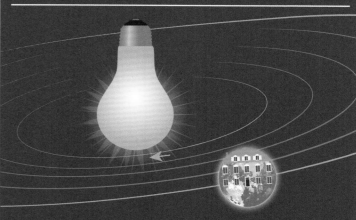

This revolution* determines the seasons, the major climate regions, and how long night and day last.

365 DAYS: THE TIME IT TAKES THE EARTH TO GO AROUND THE SUN.

584 MILLION MI.: THE DISTANCE THE EARTH TRAVELS TO GO AROUND THE SUN.

⑤

ADJUSTABLE LIGHTING

Six months

Between March and September, the Sun shines all day and night on the North Pole, and the same phenomenon occurs at the South Pole between September and March.

ITS CALLED THE POLAR DAY: THE SUN NEVER SETS!

NORTH POLE

NORTHERN HEMISPHERE

EQUATOR

Twelve hours

The equator is an imaginary line that runs around the middle of the Earth at the same distance from both poles. Gabon, Indonesia, and Ecuador are among about 10 countries on this line. Day and night always last the same amount of time here, with 12 hours of light all year round, in every season.

Between nine and sixteen hours

For countries in the Northern Hemisphere (the United States, Japan, etc.), the length of the day varies with each season. Days get longer in summer, with up to 16 hours of light on the summer solstice (June 21). Then the days grow shorter in winter, with only nine hours of Sun on the shortest day of the year, the winter solstice (December 21).

⑥

THE SMOKE DETECTOR

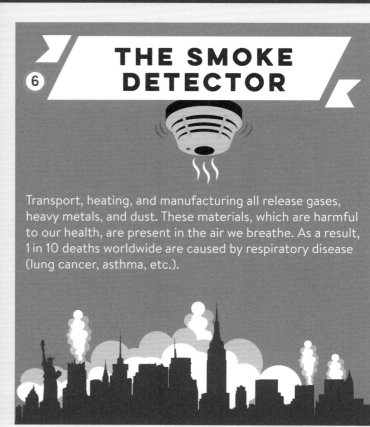

Transport, heating, and manufacturing all release gases, heavy metals, and dust. These materials, which are harmful to our health, are present in the air we breathe. As a result, 1 in 10 deaths worldwide are caused by respiratory disease (lung cancer, asthma, etc.).

THE LIVING ROOMS

THE CONTINENTS

JUST UNDER 58 MILLION SQ.MI.:

THE SURFACE **AREA OF TODAY'S** CONTINENTS.

BACK TO THE LOFT?

②

Today's continents are still moving at a rate of up to 2.8 in. per year. If these movements continue at the current rate, there could be a single continent again in about 250 million years! But not all scientists foresee the same scenario:

FROM 0.4 TO 2.8 IN. PER YEAR
← →

① **AN EVOLVING HOME**

Everything on Earth changes, including the shape and number of continents! Because of plate tectonics, the Earth's land masses are constantly moving around and changing shape.

PANGAEA

Panthalassan Ocean

The old loft

More than 250 million years ago, there was just one continent, Pangaea, surrounded by a single ocean.

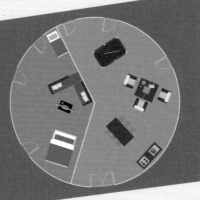

LAURASIA
Tethys Sea
GONDWANA
Panthalassan Ocean

The two-room apartment

Pangaea gradually broke into two land masses, separated by a newly formed ocean, the Tethys.

The current house

The two continents continued to split apart...

OCEANIA · ASIA · N. & S. AMERICA · ANTARCTICA · EUROPE · AFRICA

SCENARIO 1
The joining of Eurasia and North America could create Amasia.

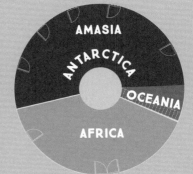

AMASIA · ANTARCTICA · OCEANIA · AFRICA

SCENARIO 2
Africa, Eurasia, and the Americas could come together to form Pangaea Ultima.

ANTARCTICA · PANGAEA ULTIMA

SCENARIO 3
As Australia, eastern Asia, and Antarctica move towards the existing continents, it could give rise to New Pangaea.

NEW PANGAEA

SIX OR SEVEN ROOMS?
Today, most Americans believe there are seven continents: North America, South America, Europe, Africa, Asia, Oceania, and Antarctica (1). But the international scientific community groups Europe and Asia into a single continent (Eurasia), for a total of six (2)! Some Europeans think of North and South America as one continent (3).

1

North America · Europe · Asia · Africa · South America · Oceania · Antarctica

2

North America · Eurasia · Africa · South America · Oceania · Antarctica

3

America · Europe · Asia · Africa · Oceania · Antarctica

DIFFERENT-SIZED ROOMS

③

THE GAME ROOM, TV ROOM, AND OFFICE
3.3 MILLION SQ. MI.
POPULATION: 40 MILLION +
16 COUNTRIES

Oceania has the lowest population of all the continents except Antarctica. It is the only continent composed entirely of islands: Australia, New Zealand, New Guinea, and more than 10,000 islands in the Pacific Ocean.

THE BIG BEDROOM
16 MILLION SQ. MI.
POPULATION: 1 BILLION
35 COUNTRIES

North and South America are connected by a narrow strip of land separating the Caribbean Sea from the Pacific Ocean. This is called the Isthmus of Panama.

A GIGANTIC DINING ROOM
17.2 MILLION SQ. MI.
POPULATION: 4 BILLION
47 COUNTRIES

Nearly 60% of the world's population lives in Asia. People living in China and India account for half of that.

THE BIGGEST AND THE MOST POPULATED CONTINENT.

OCEANIA

N. & S. AMERICA

ASIA

ANTARCTICA

EUROPE

AFRICA

A BIG LIVING ROOM
11.7 MILLION SQ. MI.
POPULATION: 1.2 BILLION +
54 COUNTRIES

Africa's population has doubled in the past 50 years.

SECOND-MOST POPULATED CONTINENT.

THE SMALL BEDROOM
4 MILLION SQ. MI.
POPULATION: 750 MILLION
45 COUNTRIES

In Europe, nearly 287 languages are spoken. But that's nothing compared to the 7,000 + languages spoken on Earth!

---

④

THE WALK-IN FREEZER

4 MILLION SQ. MI.

POPULATION: LESS THAN
1,800 A YEAR.

57.5 × UK =

98% OF THE "WHITE CONTINENT" IS COVERED IN ICE.

Antarctica is the coldest and windiest continent and has winds of up to 198 mph. For this reason, humans have never settled here, leaving the continent untouched by civilization. The few inhabitants are mostly scientists on research missions, living and working temporarily in about 50 research stations.

ANTARCTICA

MORE THAN 2.9 MILLION SQ. MI.

32 × UK

=

AUSTRALIA IS THE BIGGEST ISLAND IN THE WORLD, FOLLOWED BY GREENLAND AND NEW GUINEA.

THE KITCHEN

FOOD RESOURCES

815 MILLION PEOPLE AROUND THE WORLD DON'T HAVE ENOUGH **FOOD TO EAT.**

THE MAIN CAUSES ARE WAR, FLOODING, AND DROUGHTS.

THE CUPBOARD

②

Chocolate is made from cocoa beans, sugar from sugar cane or beets, and flour from wheat or chestnuts. Most of what we eat is grown on land.

90% DARK

SUGAR

FLOUR

90% OF OUR FOOD COMES FROM JUST EIGHT ANIMAL SPECIES (COWS, CHICKENS, PIGS, SHEEP, ETC.) AND 15 PLANT SPECIES (CORN, WHEAT, RICE, ETC.). THOSE SPECIES INCLUDE A HUGE RANGE OF BREEDS OR VARIETIES.

THE REFRIGERATOR

①

People in prehistoric times fed themselves by hunting, fishing, and gathering wild fruits or vegetables. Then, about 10,000 years ago, humans began farming and raising livestock.

Fish

Half of the fish consumed worldwide comes from fish farms and the other half comes from fishing. But because of fishing trawlers (large boats that use huge nets to rake the ocean floor), there are fewer and fewer fish in the ocean.

This invasive fishing technique is highly criticized because it has contributed to the extinction of many species (of sea turtles, sharks, etc.), but also because nearly 10 million tons of dead fish are thrown back into the sea each year if they're too small or can't be sold.

Meat and eggs

Much of the meat we eat comes from animals (cows, pigs, sheep, etc.) that are often raised in huge numbers and in bad conditions. Poultry (chickens, ducks, etc.) makes up more than 80% of these animals.

MORE THAN 2 TRILLION EGGS ARE EATEN EVERY YEAR WORLDWIDE.

Dairy

We also raise cows, sheep, and goats for their milk, which is used to make cheese, yogurt, and butter.

Fruit and vegetables

Worldwide, we grow and eat more than a hundred varieties of fruit and vegetables. But over the past 100 years, more than 75% of apple, tomato, and melon varieties has disappeared because farmers prefer high-yielding varieties. This narrowing down of varieties depletes the soil and makes plants weaker.

GMO—DANGER?

③

The three most commonly grown plants in the world are sugar cane, corn, and wheat.

The majority of the world's corn is eaten by livestock. Corn is also one of the most common GMOs (genetically modified organisms), together with canola and soybeans.

GMOs are plants that have been genetically modified to protect them from harmful insects and diseases. Many scientists are concerned about the increasing use of these plants: they may have negative effects on people's health and on the environment. However, the risks they pose have not been proven.

SWITCH ON THE EXTRACTOR HOOD!

④

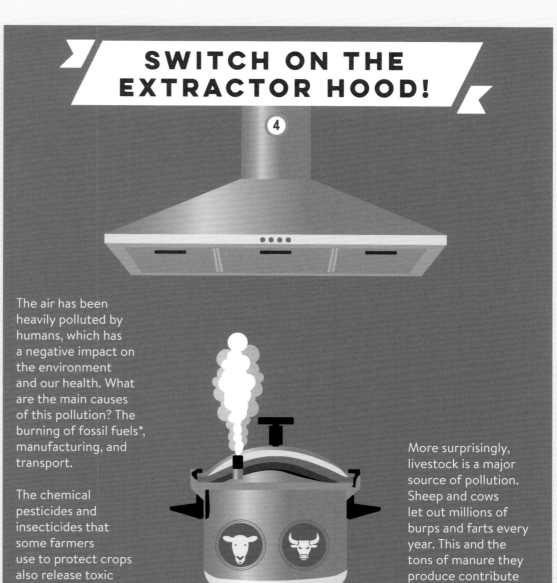

The air has been heavily polluted by humans, which has a negative impact on the environment and our health. What are the main causes of this pollution? The burning of fossil fuels*, manufacturing, and transport.

The chemical pesticides and insecticides that some farmers use to protect crops also release toxic particles into the air.

More surprisingly, livestock is a major source of pollution. Sheep and cows let out millions of burps and farts every year. This and the tons of manure they produce contribute to global warming*!

PUTTING A STOP TO WASTE

⑤

To fight food waste, some organizations collect expired food from supermarkets or unsellable (but perfectly good) fruit and vegetables from farmers. Some restaurants offer their customers the opportunity to take home leftovers in doggie bags. And just imagine the dishes you can make with leftovers!

HOW SHOULD WE CLEAN THE KITCHEN?

⑥

All over the world, farmers and consumers are looking for ways to feed everyone without polluting the Earth!

41.2 TONS OF FOOD ARE **WASTED** EVERY SECOND ON **EARTH.**

Should people eat insects instead of meat, become vegetarian, or buy only organic, chemical-free food?

THE
UTILITY ROOM

GARBAGE AND MEDICATION

EVERY YEAR, 20 BILLION TONS OF GARBAGE ARE DUMPED INTO THE OCEAN, 80% OF WHICH COMES FROM THE LAND!

Radioactive waste

Nuclear-power plants produce electricity while emitting very little greenhouse gas*. But the reactors in these power plants create radioactive waste, some of which can be very harmful to our health and the environment for millions of years to come! Since it is impossible to recycle or otherwise dispose of it, the waste is carried in special trucks and then stored in containers more than 650 ft. underground.

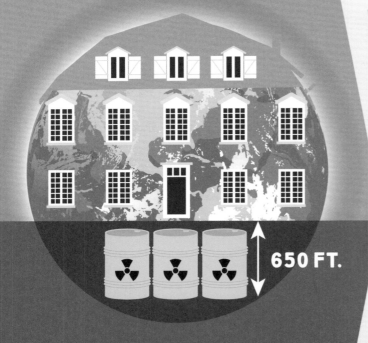

650 FT.

BUT NO ONE KNOWS IF THESE CONTAINERS WILL BE DURABLE ENOUGH.

---

① **THE TRASH CAN**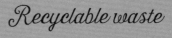

Every day, humans create more than 22 billion lb. of waste on Earth...

Recyclable waste

To prevent the planet from turning into a giant trash can, certain kinds of waste (glass and plastic bottles, cardboard packaging, cans, etc.) can be collected at recycling centers. They are then transported to factories where they are turned into new products, such as recycled paper, shopping carts, or bicycles.

FOR THIS SYSTEM TO WORK, YOU HAVE TO SORT YOUR WASTE AT HOME AND PUT IT IN THE CORRECT RECYCLING BIN!

Hazardous waste

Lacquers, batteries, glue, and paint contain harmful substances that can damage your health and the environment. When the items can't be recycled, they are incinerated or stored in protected facilities and then destroyed.

THIS TYPE OF WASTE MUST BE DROPPED OFF AT A GARBAGE COLLECTION CENTER.

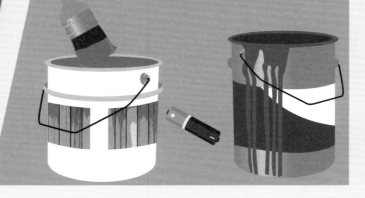

COMPOST
②

Most of what ends up in the trash can be turned into compost instead, with the help of bacteria, microfungi, and worms. This very rich soil can then be used as a natural fertilizer to feed plants.

COFFEE GROUNDS

EGG-SHELLS

PEELINGS

PAPER TISSUES

A SMALLER TRASH CAN!

(3)

CAN WE PRODUCE LESS TRASH? YES!

We can repair things instead of throwing them away.

Buying secondhand clothes and toys can save money and give items a new lease on life.

Bulk food (candy, dried fruit, cereals, etc.) is more commonly available in stores. Buying in bulk eliminates the need for packaging, which takes energy to produce and inevitably ends up in the trash.

720 MILLION CELL PHONES ARE THROWN AWAY EACH YEAR WORLDWIDE.

BULK ITEMS

(4) THE MEDICATION CABINET

Medication derived from plants

Many drugs are made from plants. Aspirin, for example, comes from the bark of the white willow tree, morphine (a painkiller) is extracted from poppies, and certain cancer treatments are made from a Chinese tree. There are still many left to discover.

ONLY 2% OF THE ACTIVE MOLECULES IN PLANTS HAVE BEEN TESTED FOR THEIR MEDICINAL PROPERTIES!

Drugs derived from animals

Scientists have been studying animal venom for several years now. Drugs that treat pain, hypertension, diabetes, cancer, and other ailments have already been made from the venom produced by porcupine fish, rattlesnakes, and Gila monsters (a large lizard). There are many more we haven't discovered yet.

Medication derived from mushrooms

Many antibiotics* come from microscopic fungi that naturally kill bacteria.

 PENICILLIN, THE WORLD'S FIRST ANTIBIOTIC*, WAS DISCOVERED IN 1928.

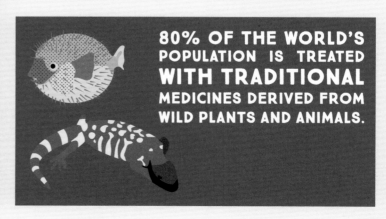

80% OF THE WORLD'S POPULATION IS TREATED WITH TRADITIONAL MEDICINES DERIVED FROM WILD PLANTS AND ANIMALS.

THE CLOSET

THE TEXTILE INDUSTRY

Cotton

Even though it requires a lot of water to grow in the right conditions, cotton is the most commonly used plant for making clothes. Strictly speaking, cotton is the fiber that surrounds the seeds of the cotton plant. The seeds are picked and sorted, then the fibers are dyed and woven.

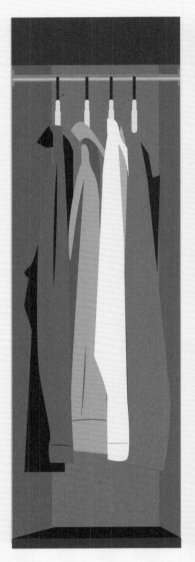

1,807 LB. OF COTTON IS MADE EVERY SECOND ON EARTH.

DRAWBACKS

Pesticides and herbicides (to treat crops), water, air, and soil pollution (from dye).

1 T-SHIRT = 2.9 LB. OF SEEDED AND CLEANED COTTON.

Petroleum

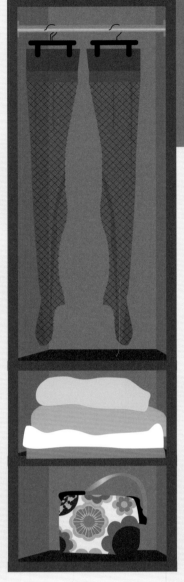

Silkworms

Without caterpillars we wouldn't have silk robes! Silk comes from the threads that the silkworm caterpillar produces to build its cocoon. This explains why silkworm farming is so popular worldwide! Silkworm farming also needs lots of plants (mulberry bushes) for these voracious caterpillars to eat.

1 SHEEP = 75 MI. OF WOOL A YEAR.

THE WARDROBE
1

Polar fleece, fake leather, nylon, polyester are all fabrics that contain synthetic fibers made from petroleum that's been pumped out of the Earth's crust. They are the most commonly used fabrics, but they are also the most damaging to the environment.

PETROLEUM

18,349 LB. OF POLYESTER IS MADE EVERY SECOND ON EARTH.

DRAWBACKS

Air and water pollution from its production, treatment, and machine washing.

Sheep, goats, etc.

All over the world, animals (sheep, goats, alpacas, etc.) are bred for the quality of their wool. Once or twice a year they are sheared (given a full-body haircut), and their wool, which grows back naturally, is collected. After it's been washed, dried, and combed, the wool can be made into yarn that's used to make sweaters, scarves, and coats.

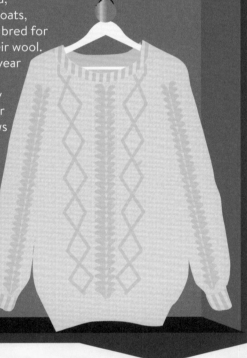

DRAWBACKS

Water pollution (from treating and dyeing), animal abuse (sheep, goats, etc.).

148 LB. OF WOOL IS PRODUCED EVERY SECOND ON EARTH.

14 LB. OF SILK IS PRODUCED EVERY SECOND ON EARTH.

DRAWBACKS

Pesticides and fertilizers (from planting), water pollution (dyes), and animal abuse (caterpillars).

THE SHOE RACK

No animals, no leather! Leather shoes, bags, belts—they're all made from animal hides (the skin taken from cows, calves, and lambs). Chromium is used to transform the skin into soft, long-lasting, waterproof leather. Chromium is both bad for the environment and damaging to your health.

OVERFLOWING DRAWERS

A lot of clothes are made in factories by children or very low-paid workers and then sold at very low prices. Because of this, lots of clothes are thrown away and replaced by new ones, even if they're still in good condition. All this waste is a major source of pollution.

MORE THAN 80 BILLION ITEMS OF NEW CLOTHING ARE SOLD WORLDWIDE EVERY YEAR!

35 WEARS: THE AVERAGE LIFESPAN OF A NEW PIECE OF CLOTHING.

THE IDEAL CLOSET

Organic

Ideally, all plants would be grown organically, without using chemical products (pesticides, fertilizers), which pollute the soil, rivers, and groundwater reserves*. Organic cotton and wild silk (where caterpillars die naturally) are already being produced.

Eco-friendly

Hemp, eucalyptus, flax, and bamboo all grow easily without pesticides and require very little water. Many clothing manufacturers use them instead of more polluting fibers such as cotton and petroleum-based synthetic fibers.

HEMP **BAMBOO**

EUCALYPTUS **FLAX**

Vintage

Instead of throwing your clothes in the trash, you can recycle them. Buying from secondhand-clothing stores saves money and reduces the pollution caused by the textile industry.

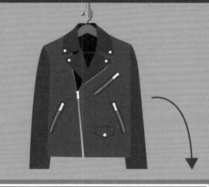

THRIFT STORE

Ethical

Sheep, goats, cows, silkworms—all these animals deserve to be raised in good conditions. Vegan* consumers take things a step further by refusing to wear clothes that are made from animals or animal products. To meet their needs, manufacturers have invented vegetable "leather" made from rubber sap or from the fiber in pineapple leaves.

THE SUNROOM

NATURAL HABITATS AND VEGETATION

LIGHTING AND WATERING

①

To grow, plants need soil, water, and light. Vegetation around the world is very different, depending on the climate and the type of the soil.

Near the poles, it is very cold all year round and the subsoil is permanently frozen. Only a few types of bushes, mosses, and lichens grow there.

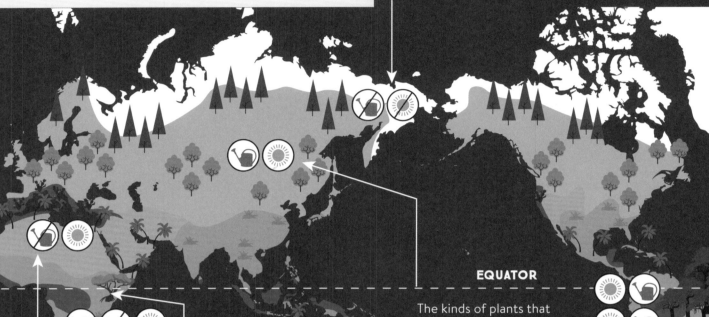

EQUATOR

The kinds of plants that grow in areas that are far from the sea (taiga, meadows, deciduous forests, etc.) are different from those that grow in mountain areas (beech and fir forests, low-growing plants), coastal areas (heaths, deciduous forests), and the Mediterranean (pine forests, scrubland).

In desert areas, plants don't have enough water, so they struggle to grow.

In tropical zones, on both sides of the equator (savanna, steppes, etc.), plants are subjected to alternating dry and wet seasons.

Near the equator, it is hot all year round and it rains a lot. This is where the most abundant and varied vegetation is found, often in dense forests.

31,000: THE NUMBER OF PLANT SPECIES **HUMANS** USE TO MAKE THEIR **MEDICINE, FOOD, FUEL, AND MATERIALS.**

TREES AND PLANTS

②

Plants play a very important role on Earth. They enrich the soil and feed the millions of animals that eat them to survive. By absorbing carbon dioxide (CO_2) from the atmosphere, they also allow us to breathe!

Trees

Several teams of botanists have counted how many tree species there are in the world. A tree is any plant with a wooden trunk that's at least 6.5 ft. tall. Anything smaller is considered a shrub. There are at least 65,065 tree species on Earth. More than half of these are found in Brazil.

Plants

Even though scientists consider trees to be plants too, this category generally refers to plants that are small in size or whose trunks or stems do not turn into wood. There are more than 390,000 species of plants, not to mention all the ones that haven't been discovered yet.

RARE PLANTS

③

For every ton (2,000 lb.) of plant material (trees, plants, flowers, etc.) that grows in the wild, humans collect 550 lb. of it to make food and clothing, or to heat, build, and decorate their homes.

550 LB.

1 IN 5 PLANTS WORLDWIDE
ARE IN DANGER OF BECOMING EXTINCT.

This explains why several plant species are in danger of disappearing in the near future. One example of this is wild orchids, which are harder and harder to find in nature.

THE LADY'S SLIPPER ORCHID, AN ENDANGERED SPECIES.

2,000
NEW PLANT SPECIES ARE DISCOVERED ON AVERAGE EVERY YEAR BY SCIENTISTS.

32
TREES ARE PLANTED EVERY SECOND WORLDWIDE.

32 TO 37 MILLION
ACRES OF VEGETATION
DISAPPEAR EVERY YEAR.
THAT'S MORE THAN A
FOOTBALL FIELD EVERY SECOND!

TROPICAL GREENHOUSE

④

In Asia and South America, tropical forests are disappearing at an alarming rate. Farmers often chop down and burn trees to make room for livestock or soybean and palm-oil crops. Trees are cut down to clear space for roads and new buildings. Forests are also destroyed for their wood so we can make furniture, paper, firewood, and build homes. This is called deforestation.

The dangers

Deforestation depletes the soil, causes many plant and animal species to become extinct, and contributes to global warming*. Forests naturally absorb carbon dioxide (CO_2), so as more more trees disappear, huge amounts of greenhouse gas* are left in the atmosphere.

The solutions

All over the world, major reforestation efforts are bringing forests back to life. In addition to this, many associations (WWF, Greenpeace, etc.) are suggesting more ways to fight deforestation. Examples include eating less meat, buying cereals and snacks that don't contain palm oil, buying recycled paper, and getting wood from sustainable forests.

THE ROOMMATES

HUMANS

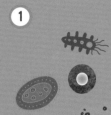

1 How did life on Earth begin? There are several theories, but no scientist knows exactly when or how it came about. The first living organisms that populated our planet probably looked like bacteria.

THEN MULTICELLULAR ORGANISMS GRADUALLY EVOLVED.

MARINE INVERTEBRATES

MARINE VERTEBRATES

TERRESTRIAL PLANTS

TERRESTRIAL ANIMALS

DINOSAURS

5 MILLION HUMANS LIVED ON EARTH IN 8,000 B.C.

7.7 BILLION HUMANS LIVE ON EARTH IN 2019.

THE CURRENT TENANTS

2

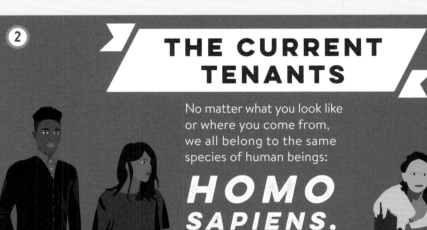

No matter what you look like or where you come from, we all belong to the same species of human beings:

HOMO SAPIENS.

For a long time, scientists thought that the first *Homo sapiens* appeared 200,000 years ago in East Africa. But the discovery in 2017 of new skeletons in Morocco proves that they emerged at least 300,000 years ago.

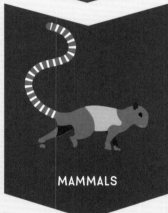
MAMMALS

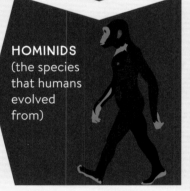
HOMINIDS (the species that humans evolved from)

TOO MANY PEOPLE IN THE HOUSE?

3

Since there are many more births than deaths, the world's population is constantly growing.

According to scientific predictions, the global population could rise from over 7.7 billion in 2019 to over 9 billion in 2050!

But with hundreds of millions of people already going hungry today, will we be able to feed everyone? Scientists say the answer is yes. But we will have to produce more food and distribute it more evenly while creating less pollution. This is a real challenge that experts all over the world are trying to tackle.

HOME MAINTENANCE

④

What needs to be fixed?

By leaving the lights on when you leave a room, wasting energy, or buying lots of things that end up in the trash, or wearing clothes that are highly polluting to make, your day-to-day actions can have a negative impact on the environment.

ENVIRONMENTAL FOOTPRINT =

The impact of human activity (farming, driving, creating waste, etc.) on the planet.

How do we fix it?

By changing our habits, we can all reduce the impact we have on the environment and help protect the future of our planet. For example, we can reduce our carbon footprint by carpooling or biking; we can reduce our electricity consumption by turning off lights and turning down the heat; and we can create less trash by repairing and recycling household items.

To calculate our environmental footprint, scientists measure the percentage of the Earth's surface that we would need to produce everything necessary to get around, eat, get dressed, and heat our homes. AND WHAT HAVE THEY DISCOVERED?

1 + 0.7

IT WOULD TAKE 1.7 EARTHS TO SUSTAIN OUR CURRENT LEVELS OF CONSUMPTION.

This is why many scientists are worried about the future of our planet.

HOME FINANCES

⑤

Are we all equal on Earth? No, there is significant inequality. Many people do not have access to safe drinking water, proper nutrition, education, or medical care. Additionally, women are often paid less than men, and often lack the same rights.

Wealth is also not evenly distributed: income inequality has been on the rise for 40 years.

42 BILLIONAIRES POSSESS AS MUCH WEALTH AS HALF OF THE WORLD'S POPULATION.

82%

82% OF THE WEALTH GENERATED IN 2017 WENT TO ONLY 1% OF THE WORLD'S POPULATION.

1992

THE RIO DE JANEIRO EARTH SUMMIT

That year, 173 countries committed to improving government policies around the world to fight against pollution, global warming*, and extinction of species.

A LIMITED LEASE

⑥

The Earth is able to sustain life because it is rich in liquid water, it has an atmosphere, and it is neither too close to the Sun nor too far from it, making it neither too hot nor too cold.

5 TO 7 BILLION YEARS

However, like all stars, the Sun has a limited timespan: it will mostly likely die in about 5 to 7 billion years from now, taking our planet with it when it goes.

Humans will disappear from Earth long before then. But according to scientific calculations, Earth will no longer be able to support human life in around 500 million years.

500 MILLION YEARS

Other organisms (insects, bacteria, etc.) will be able to live here for 1.75 billion more years at least. After that, even the most resilient microorganisms will become extinct.

1.75 BILLION YEARS

THE ROOMMATES

ANIMALS

24,307 SPECIES WORLDWIDE ARE AT RISK OF BECOMING EXTINCT.

13% OF BIRDS

26% OF MAMMALS

42% OF AMPHIBIANS

30% OF STINGRAYS AND SHARKS

2 MILLION: THE NUMBER OF KNOWN ANIMAL SPECIES ON EARTH.

THERE COULD BE BETWEEN 6 AND 28 MILLION SPECIES WE HAVEN'T DISCOVERED YET!

Today

Nearly 50% of all animal species, including those in the ocean, could disappear by 2050. Hunting, fishing, pollution, the destruction of habitats, the spread of invasive species (which disrupt their new habitat), and global warming* are to blame.

AN UNCERTAIN LEASE

①

There have been five major extinction phases since life first appeared on Earth. They lasted hundreds of thousands, if not millions, of years. A sixth wave of extinction is happening right now. But this time, animals are dying off 100 to 1,000 times faster than before.

443 MILLION YEARS AGO

Nearly 85% of marine life became extinct. The possible cause: a major freeze that caused the ocean levels to go down.

85%

359 MILLION YEARS AGO

Almost 75% of animal species (especially marine) became extinct. The possible cause: either an ice age or a massive influx of terrestrial plant waste that led to a huge increase in algae and bacteria in the sea.

75%

252 MILLION YEARS AGO

More than 90% of marine species and 70% of land species became extinct. The possible causes: A microorganism that suddenly began multiplying in huge numbers, releasing a huge amount of methane into the atmosphere. Or a meteorite that hit Earth, triggering a series of volcanic eruptions that emitted metals and toxic gases into the air.

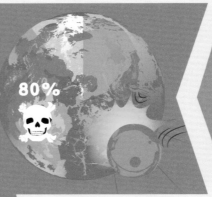

80%

201 MILLION YEARS AGO

50% of animal species became extinct.

50%

The possible cause: a meteorite fell and/or volcanoes erupted, releasing toxic gases that led to global warming*.

66 MILLION YEARS AGO

60 to 80% of animal species (including the dinosaurs) became extinct. The possible cause: a meteorite hit Earth, causing tsunamis, toxic rains, and a period of global cooling.

60%–80%

DIVIDING UP CHORES

(2)

The term biodiversity* applies to all animals, plants, bacteria, or fungi on Earth. These organisms are all adapted to their natural habitat (desert, forest, sea, etc.) and interact with each other: this is known as an ecosystem*.

Earthworms enrich the soil we grow our food in. Without them, the soil is depleted.

Honeybees, bumblebees, and butterflies pollinate many flowering plants, which produce much of the fruit and vegetables we eat. Their extinction threatens plants' ability to reproduce, and therefore our ability to eat.

Sharks eat fish, and some of those fish eat tiny algae (phytoplankton). This algae isn't just fish food, though—phytoplankton produce much of the oxygen needed to maintain a balance in the ocean and everywhere on Earth. Over time, a loss of phytoplankton could lead to a mass extinction of marine life and turn the ocean into a dead zone.

This is just one of many examples. As biodiversity* declines, it could cause whole ecosystems* to collapse. The health of our planet depends greatly on the creatures that inhabit it.

SHARING THE LIVING SPACE

(3)

Global warming*, hunting, large-scale fishing and, more generally, the overexploitation of resources and over-hunting of animals are just a few of the dangers faced by animals. But the destruction of natural habitats is by far the biggest cause of species extinction. Every time humans destroy a meadow or forest to plant crops, or build factories, roads, and houses, the animals that were living there tend to die.

LIVING IN HARMONY

(4)

How?

Faced with the staggering number of endangered species, scientists sometimes have to consider which ones to save first: this is called "conservation triage." The species that receive the most protection are often the most endangered, or the most unique, or they are "umbrella species"—animals whose protection leads to that of other animals.

There are many ways to protect animals:
• By preserving their habitats by creating natural reserves.
• By banning poaching and overfishing.
• By introducing endangered species back into their natural environment.

And on top of that, everyone can play their part by not using chemicals in their gardens, so as to protect insects, and by not littering.

Why?

Not only do animals contribute to the well-being of our planet, they are also the source of much of our food and medicine. Many of our technological inventions and innovations are also inspired by plants and animals in the wild. Plus, there are lots of species we haven't discovered yet—species that could be of great benefit to us some day.

VACATION HOMES

LIFE ON ANOTHER PLANET?

6 MONTHS: THE TIME IT CURRENTLY TAKES TO GET TO MARS.

WHY WOULD WE MOVE?

①

Moving to another planet would be a solution if our planet got too polluted or too hot, or ran out of natural resources. You need to plan that sort of move in advance!

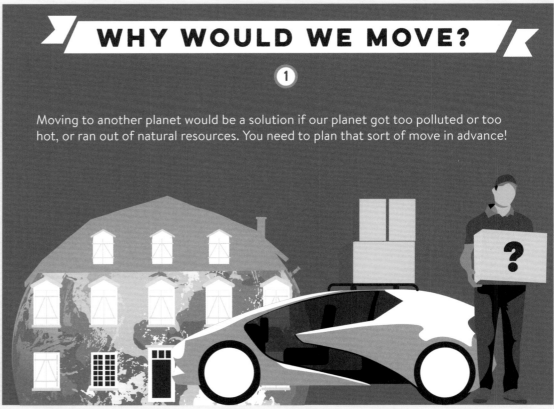

HABITABLE HOMES

②

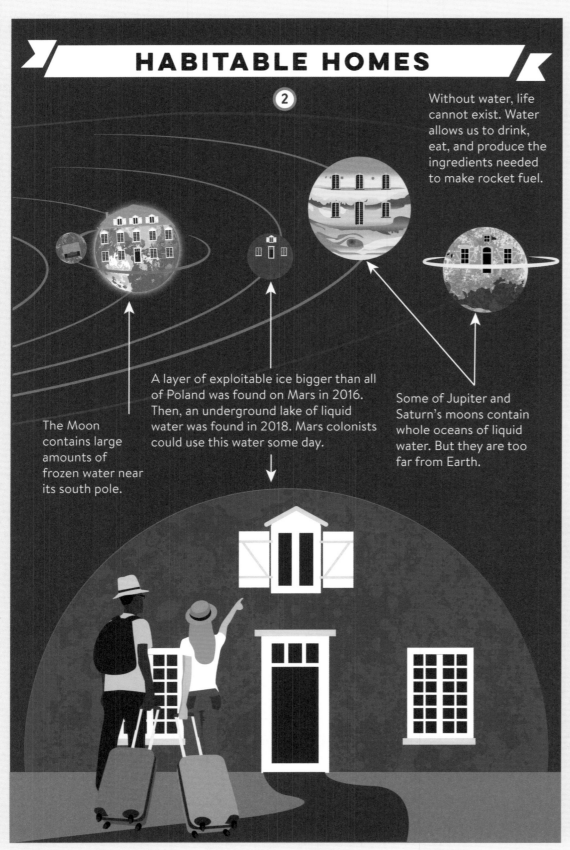

Without water, life cannot exist. Water allows us to drink, eat, and produce the ingredients needed to make rocket fuel.

A layer of exploitable ice bigger than all of Poland was found on Mars in 2016. Then, an underground lake of liquid water was found in 2018. Mars colonists could use this water some day.

The Moon contains large amounts of frozen water near its south pole.

Some of Jupiter and Saturn's moons contain whole oceans of liquid water. But they are too far from Earth.

THE MODEL HOUSE

③

If humans were to settle on Mars tomorrow, what would their lives be like? To find out, scientists have carried out several missions where they tried to recreate living conditions on Mars.

From 2015 to 2016, a team of six volunteers spent a whole year locked in a dome built on a desert volcano in Hawaii. The dome was only 36 ft. wide and 20 ft. high. The participants were only allowed to go outside dressed in spacesuits. They also ate nothing but dehydrated food and had an ultra-slow Internet connection.

THE CONCLUSION?
Despite the isolation and the lack of fresh air, everyone left the dome in good health and willing to recreate the experience on Mars.

SHORT TERM: SMALL PROJECTS IN THE WORKS

On the Moon

THE PROBLEM
The Moon is subject to extreme temperatures (as hot as 257°F during the day and as cold as -283°F at night). The Moon has no atmosphere (which we need to breathe) and no magnetic shield to protect it from solar wind.

On Mars

THE PROBLEM
Mars is a cold planet (-81°F on average), and its atmosphere is 100 times thinner than the Earth's. The air on Mars is mostly made up of carbon dioxide (difficult to breathe). Mars also does not have a magnetic shield.

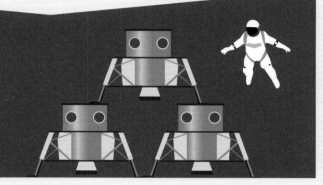

THE SOLUTION
To live there, scientists have suggested turning the old lava tunnels on the Moon into tightly sealed underground passageways filled with a man-made atmosphere!

THE SOLUTION
The first settlers will have to live in whatever modules they bring from Earth. But these spaces could then be expanded by building airtight structures. Just like on the Moon, though, it will be impossible to go outside without a spacesuit.

LONG TERM: MAJOR OPERATIONS

How to live on Mars without a spacesuit or an oxygen mask? Scientists propose putting a huge magnetic shield in orbit around the planet to deflect the solar wind. This would restore its atmosphere and make it a warmer and more habitable place. The most popular idea is terra-forming. This would involve changing the conditions on the planet to make it more similar to Earth.

The construction phases

1. STARTING IN THE FIRST YEAR
We would need to build chemical factories that pollute Mars by pumping huge quantities of greenhouse gases* into the air. These would thicken the atmosphere and warm the planet.

2. IN 100 TO 300 YEARS
Once the planet has heated up, the ice melted, the atmosphere thickened, and lakes and rivers have reappeared, we would then need to dump microbes on land and establish plant life in order to add oxygen to the air. Then people could ditch the spacesuits. A mask, an oxygen tank, and a light suit would be enough to protect them.

Then we would put a gigantic mirror in orbit around Mars in order to capture the Sun's heat and raise the air temperature even more. With this, people should be able to walk around in spacesuits.

A 3D PRINTER ON THE MOON?
The moon could also act as a manned space outpost that sends missions to Mars. To avoid having to send building materials from Earth, the European Space Agency (ESA) is considering using a 3D printer to build the outpost—with raw materials mined directly on the Moon!

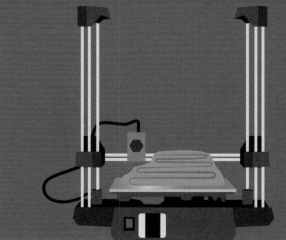

3. IN 1,000 TO 10,000 YEARS
There would be enough oxygen in the atmosphere for it to resemble Earth. People could then breathe and walk around freely.

THE NEIGHBORS

EXOPLANETS AND EXTRATERRESTRIAL LIFE

IS THERE LIFE BEYOND EARTH?

Back in the fourth century B.C., the Greek philosopher Epicurus declared: "There is an infinite number of worlds like ours and an infinite number of worlds that aren't like ours."

1 LIGHT-YEAR = ABOUT 5.8 TRILLION MILES

OUR CLOSEST NEIGHBORS

②

THE SUN

ROCKY PLANETS*

MERCURY

VENUS

EARTH

MARS

JUPITER

SATURN

URANUS

NEPTUNE

GASEOUS PLANETS

Circling the Sun

Earth is one of eight planets in our solar system. It revolves around the Sun, just like the three other rocky planets* (Mercury, Venus, and Mars) and the four gaseous planets (Jupiter, Saturn, Uranus, and Neptune). Life could exist wherever scientists believe there may be liquid water, such as on Europa and Ganymede (two of Jupiter's moons), and on Enceladus (one of Saturn's moons).

ARE OTHER HOMES INHABITED?

①

Since 1995, scientists have discovered more than 3,700 exoplanets. Most are gaseous planets, but a few are rocky planets*. Are they populated with living beings? Maybe. Some small planets are located in the "habitable zone," meaning they're neither too close nor too far from their stars. If these planets contain liquid water they could sustain life!

STAR

HABITABLE ZONE

EXOPLANET

1995: ASTRONOMERS DETECTED THE FIRST EXOPLANET, 51 PEGASI B.

4 DAYS

LOCATED 50 LIGHT-YEARS FROM EARTH, IT COMPLETES THE ORBIT AROUND ITS STAR IN JUST OVER 4 DAYS.

200 TO 400 BILLION: THE NUMBER OF STARS IN OUR GALAXY, THE MILKY WAY.

THERE COULD BE ONE OR MORE PLANETS ORBITING EACH OF THESE STARS. THESE ARE CALLED EXOPLANETS.

Circling Proxima Centauri

The star closest to the Sun, Proxima Centauri, is 4.2 light-years away. Orbiting it is Proxima b—the closest-known exoplanet to the Earth! Ever since it was discovered in 2016, it has sparked a lot of interest from the scientific community.

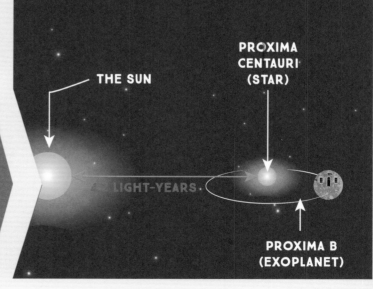

THE SUN

PROXIMA CENTAURI (STAR)

LIGHT-YEARS

PROXIMA B (EXOPLANET)

IT WOULD TAKE 60,000 YEARS TO REACH PROXIMA B USING THE FASTEST SPACE PROBE WE HAVE TODAY (AVERAGE SPEED: 9 MI./S).

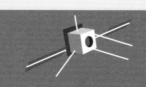

IS ANYONE OUT THERE?

③

1959: American physicists created the SETI (Search for Extraterrestrial Intelligence) program.

THE GOAL?
To use any and all technology available to us (radio telescopes, computers, etc.) to try to pick up an extraterrestrial signal that would prove that intelligent life exists beyond Earth. As of today, no clear signal has been detected.

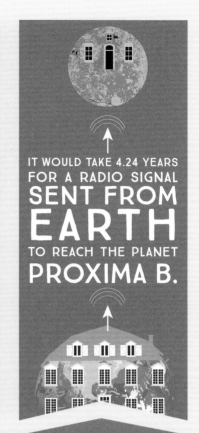

IT WOULD TAKE 4.24 YEARS FOR A RADIO SIGNAL **SENT FROM EARTH** TO REACH THE PLANET **PROXIMA B.**

MEETING OUR NEIGHBORS?

④

If we can't go visit them...

The number of exoplanets we've discovered is still tiny compared to the number of stars in the Milky Way. Plus, no spacecraft capable of reaching them currently exists.

...then we'll send them messages!

METI (Messaging Extraterrestrial Intelligence) is a group of researchers working on sending messages (using radio waves, lasers, etc.) to an alien civilization. But scientists are divided on this topic: while some believe it is in our best interests to discover new life-forms, others are worried about it.

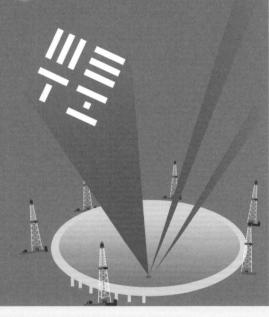

What if they came to visit us?

Most scientists believe that there is life beyond Earth. So why haven't we been contacted by aliens yet? According to Jean-Claude Ribes and Guy Monnet, two French researchers, there are several explanations:

1. No alien civilization has developed a spaceship capable of getting to Earth.

2. Alien civilizations are already traveling around space, they just haven't reached us yet.

3. Alien civilizations have already found us and are observing us without us knowing it.

4. Alien civilizations are much older than ours. Not only have they already discovered us, but they were the ones who created humankind!

INDEX

A

Agriculture 14, 45
Air 6, 11, 22, 25, 29, 32, 38, 40, 41
Alien 43
Altitude 18
Aluminum 7, 8, 16, 17
Amphibian 38
Animal 14, 15, 28, 29, 31, 32, 33,
34, 35, 36, 38, 39, 45
Antibiotic 31, 45
Asteroid 7, 8
Astronomer 42
Atmosphere 8, 11, 17, 21, 22, 24, 25,
34, 35, 37, 38, 41, 45
Aurora Australis 11
Aurora Borealis 11

B

Bacteria 15, 25, 30, 31, 36, 37, 38, 39, 45
Bauxite 17
Big Bang 6
Biodiversity 15, 23, 39, 45
Bird 23, 38

C

Calcite 16
Carbon dioxide 8, 22, 24, 34, 35, 41
Chemical product 33
Climate 14, 15, 17, 22, 24, 25, 34
Coal 10, 16, 17, 24, 45
Comet 7, 8
Compost 30
Conservation triage 39
Consumption 37
Continent 12, 18, 23, 26, 27
Copper 16
Core 8, 10, 11, 24
Cyclone 22, 24

D

Deforestation 35
Degassing 8, 45
Desert 34, 39, 40
Dinosaur 36, 38
Drought 21, 24, 28

E

Earth's crust 8, 10, 12, 13, 14, 16, 19, 20, 32
Earthquake 10, 12, 13

Ecosystem 39, 45
Electricity 10, 16, 17, 30, 37
Endangered species 35, 39
Energy 13, 17, 24, 31, 37
Environment 15, 17, 20, 24, 29, 30,
32, 33, 37, 39, 45
Environmental footprint 37
Equator 14, 25, 34
Erosion 18, 45
Eruption 17, 19, 38, 45
Exoplanet 42, 43
Extinction (species) 24, 28, 37, 38, 39
Extraterrestrial 42, 43

F

Farming 14, 15, 21, 28, 32, 37
Fault line 13
Fertilizer 15, 23, 30, 32, 33, 45
Fishing 23, 28, 38, 39
Flooding 15, 28
Flower 35, 39
Food 15, 18, 28, 29, 31, 34, 35, 36, 39, 40, 45
Forest 14, 19, 34, 35, 39
Fuel 34, 40

G

Galaxy 8, 42
Garbage collection center 30
Garden 15, 39
Gas 7, 11, 13, 19, 24, 25, 45
 - greenhouse 24, 25, 30, 35, 41, 45
 - natural 16, 17, 19, 45
 - toxic 22, 38
Gaseous planet 7, 42, 45
Glaciation 25
Glacier 20, 21, 23, 24
Global warming 21, 22, 24, 29, 35, 37, 38, 39, 45
GMO 29
Gravity 6, 7, 45
Greenhouse effect 24
Groundwater reserve 15, 20, 23, 33, 45

H

Habitat 38, 39
Health 15, 22, 23, 25, 29, 30, 33, 39, 40, 45
Hominid 36
Homo sapiens 36
Human 13, 14, 15, 20, 22, 24, 27, 28, 29, 30,
34, 35, 36, 37, 39, 40, 43, 45
Humanity 18
Hunting 28, 38, 39
Hurricane 22, 24
Hydrogen 24, 45

I

Ice 24, 25, 27, 38, 40, 41

Iceberg 20
Inequality 37
Insect 29, 37, 39
Invasive species 38
Iron 7, 8, 10, 14, 16

J

Jupiter 7, 40, 42

K

Kaolinite 16

L

Lake 20, 21, 40, 41
Late Heavy Bombardment 7
Lava 7, 19, 41
Lead 16
Life 4, 11, 15, 35, 36, 37, 38,
39, 40, 41, 42, 43
Light 24, 25, 34, 37
Light-year 8, 42
Lighting 24, 25, 34
Limestone 16
Livestock 24, 28, 29, 35

M

Magma 13, 17, 19
Magnetic shield 11, 41
Magnitude 13
Mammal 36, 38
 - marine 23
Mantle 10, 11, 12, 13, 17, 19
Manufacturing 24, 25, 29, 45
Marble 16
Mars 7, 40, 41, 42
Medicine 31, 34, 39, 45
Mercury 7, 8, 42
Metal 10, 16, 17, 25, 38, 45
Meteorite 8, 38
Methane 24, 38
Microbe 41
Microorganism 37, 38
Milky Way 7, 8, 42, 43
Minerals 14, 15, 16, 45
Moho 10
Moon 9, 10, 40, 41, 42
Mountain 18, 19, 34, 45
Mushroom 31

N

Natural habitat 34, 39
Nature 35, 45
Nebula 7
Neptune 7, 42

44

Nickel 7, 8, 10
Nitrogen 11
Northern Lights 11
Nuclear-power plant 30

Ocean 8, 11, 12, 20, 21, 22, 23, 26,
27, 28, 30, 38, 39, 40, 45
Ocean current 22, 23
Oil 16, 17, 23, 24, 45
Organic 14, 15, 29, 33
Organism 14, 15, 16, 29, 36, 37, 39, 45
- multicellular 36
Overexploitation 39
Overfishing 39
Oxygen 7, 8, 11, 19, 22, 39, 41

Pangaea 26
Pedology 14
People 9, 13, 17, 18, 20, 21, 23, 27,
28, 29, 36, 37, 41, 45
Permaculture 15, 45
Pesticide 15, 23, 29, 32, 33, 45
Phytoplankton 22, 39
Plain 18
Plant 14, 15, 16, 28, 29, 30, 31, 32,
33, 34, 35, 36, 38, 39, 45
Plant life 41, 45
Plate tectonics 12, 26
Plateau 18
Poaching 39
Polar day 25
Pole 11, 25, 34, 40
- North 6, 20, 25
- South 6, 20, 25
Pollution 15, 17, 22, 23, 29, 32, 33, 37, 38
Population 18, 21, 27, 31, 36, 37
Prairie 14
Protection 39

Quartz 16

Rain 15, 21, 23, 34, 38
Recycling 15, 17, 30, 37
Recycling center 30
Reforestation 35
Resources 16, 28, 39, 40
Revolution 25, 45
River 6, 18, 20, 21, 23, 33, 41
Rock 8, 10, 11, 12, 13, 14,
16, 17, 18, 19, 45
Rocky planet 7, 42, 45

Satellite 6, 8, 9, 11
Saturn 7, 40, 42
Savanna 14, 34, 45
Scrubland 34
Sea 13, 18, 20, 21, 22, 23, 24,
26, 27, 28, 34, 38, 39
Season 25, 34
Seed 32
Seismograph 13
Silicon 7, 8
Soil 14, 15, 28, 30, 32,
33, 34, 35, 39, 45
Solar system 8, 42
Solar wind 11, 24, 41
Solstice 25
Southern Lights 11
Space 6, 11, 20, 24, 41, 43
Space probe 9, 42
Star 6, 7, 8, 24, 37, 42, 43, 45
Steppe 34
Subsoil 14, 34
Sun 6, 7, 8, 11, 17, 21, 22,
24, 25, 37, 41, 42

Taiga 34
Tectonic plate 12, 13, 19
Temperature 7, 8, 10, 22, 23, 24, 41, 45
Terraforming 41
Thermonuclear bomb 24, 45
Threat 23, 39
Transportation 45
Tree 31, 34, 35
Tsunami 13, 38

Umbrella species 39
Universe 6, 8
Uranus 7, 42

Vegan 33, 45
Venus 7, 8, 42
Volcano 13, 17, 19, 38, 40

Waste 15, 19, 23, 24, 29,
30, 33, 37, 38
- hazardous 30
- radioactive 30
- recyclable 30
Water 6, 7, 8, 11, 14, 15, 17, 20, 21, 22,
23, 24, 32, 33, 34, 37, 40, 42, 45
- drinking 15, 20, 21, 23, 37
- fresh 15, 20, 21
Wealth 37
Wind 17, 19, 23, 24, 27, 45

Zinc 16

GLOSSARY

• ANTIBIOTIC
A medicine that kills bacteria, particularly bacteria that make people sick.

• BIODIVERSITY
The variety of both animal and plant life in a specific place, or in the whole world.

• CONDENSATION
When a gas or vapor changes into a liquid state.

• DEGASSING
This happens when gas that is trapped in molten rock is released during a volcanic eruption.

• ECOSYSTEM
A complex network of interactions between a physical environment (the savanna, the ocean, etc.) and all the organisms that live there.

• EROSION
This is when a mountain gets slowly broken down by water and wind.

• FOSSIL FUELS
Fuels that are derived from coal, oil, or natural gas.

• GLOBAL WARMING
This is the increase in the average temperature of the oceans and atmosphere on Earth.

• GRAVITY
This is the force of attraction between two objects containing large amounts of dense matter.

• GREENHOUSE GASES
The gases that are emitted naturally, but they are also produced by humans and their actions (transportation, manufacturing, agriculture). These gases end up in the Earth's atmosphere and warm the planet.

• GROUNDWATER RESERVE
This is a layer of underground water that exists in the rock deep below the soil.

• PERMACULTURE
This is a form of agriculture that imitates nature, allowing farmers to grow food without chemicals (fertilizers, pesticides, etc.).

• REVOLUTION
A revolution refers to the time it takes for an object (such as a planet) to make a complete circle around another object (such as a star).

• ROCKY PLANET
Unlike gaseous planets, which do not have a solid surface, the rocky planets are composed of rocks and metals.

• THERMONUCLEAR BOMB
An atomic bomb made with hydrogen, a highly flammable gas.

• VEGAN
A vegan does not consume any animal products or products tested on animals. They dress, feed, bathe, and medicate themselves entirely with plant- and mineral-based products.

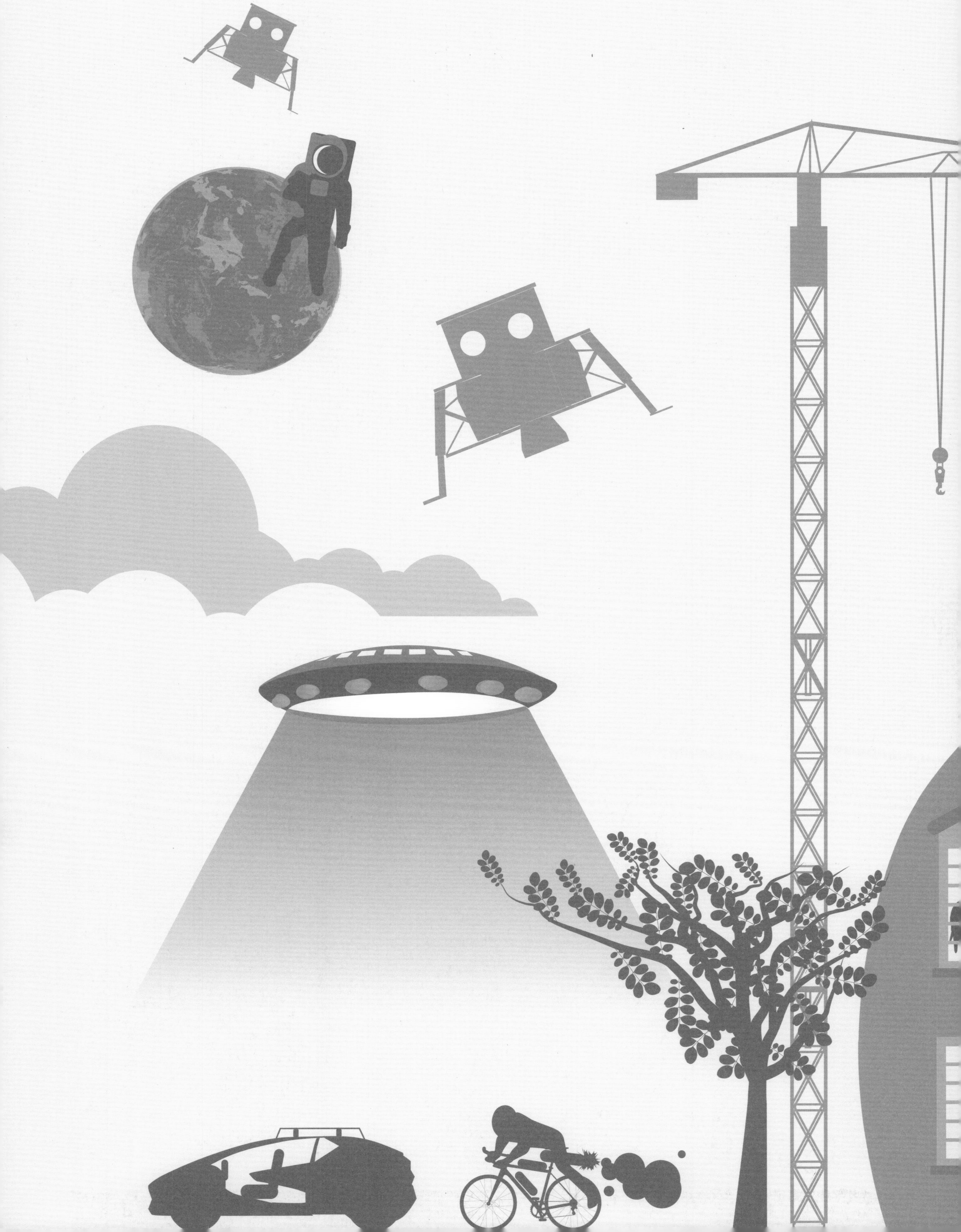